The Freedmen's Quandary

Crossroads of Tribal Identity in Indian Country

By Hodalee Scott Sewell

Published by Backintyme Publishing
Crofton, Kentucky, U.S.A.

Copyright @ 2019 by Backintyme Publishing
ALL RIGHTS RESERVED
1341 Grapevine Rd.
Crofton, KY. 42217
Website: www.backintyme.biz
Email: backintyme@mehrapublishing.com
Printed United States of America
February 2019
ISBN- 978-0-939479-55-9

Cover Art by: T-riffic Design

THE FREEDMEN'S QUANDARY

CROSSROADS OF TRIBAL IDENTITY IN INDIAN COUNTRY

BY HODALEE SCOTT SEWELL

"An Indian is an Indian regardless of the degree of Indian blood or which little government card they do or do not possess."

-Wilma Mankiller; Principal Chief of the Cherokee Nation of Oklahoma

"We might speak our language, we might look like Indians and sound like Indians, but we won't be Indians."

- Russell Means; American Indian Movement (AIM) activist and libertarian political activist, actor, writer, and musician.

"An Indian is someone who thinks of themselves as an Indian. But that's not so easy to do and one has to earn the entitlement somehow. You have to have a certain experience of the world in order to formulate this idea. I consider myself an Indian; I've had the experience of an Indian. I know how my father saw the world, and his father before him."

-Pulitzer Prize-winning Kiowa author N. Scott Momaday

"It is immoral and unethical for any lawyer to advocate for or contribute to the divestment or restriction of the American indigenous right of tribal citizenship, without equal protection at law or due process of law or an effective remedy for the violation of such rights."

- United Nations Declaration on the Rights of Indigenous Peoples

INTRODUCTION

Over the last several decades I have had the privilege of meeting and getting to know the struggle of many people in several communities of the Creek and Cherokee Nations in Oklahoma, individuals of mixed African and American Indian ancestry, who have been laboring to preserve and continue their identity as Native Americans of their respective nations. During that time as well a DNA test revealed that the oral history stories of my own family, as well as the general opinion of our tribal community's north Florida neighbors that we "Dominickers" as we were called, were of some black ancestry were shown to be correct. Those familiar with the history of the south, and of Indian Territory, are rarely surprised when people from native communities show some African lineages through genealogical or genetic research. The histories of the Indians, Europeans, and Africans have been intertwined for several centuries and many people today share common ancestries originating to all three.

For those less familiar with southern history this may be surprising, but the introduction of inexpensive DNA tests has revealed the true extent that most Americans likely share ancestries with neighbors they may perceive as being of another race; indeed, many people are surprised to hear that nearly a quarter of the southern "white" population show recent African ancestry, so how much more so would the Indian societies from the region who often willingly took outsiders into tribal communities. For the Five Tribes of Oklahoma today, that process of mixing and assimilating others has been ongoing for nearly five hundred years.

Throughout those many centuries since contact, it was common for tribes to take in refugees, adopt captives, and define tribal identity in terms of their past societal and cultural patterns, not tribal rolls, regulations, and paperwork that would come to shape tribal identity in more recent generations. The future of the unique identity as the people indigenous to the continent is extremely important to many Native Americans individuals and communities, which can cause a conservative view of tribal belonging, and a sense of foreboding with the continuous change that often sweeps across Indian Country with the changing politics of the country.

In my travels I was privileged to meet and talk with American Indian Movement Activist Russell Means on two occasions. He would many times directly address his concerns with the eroding "Indian way of life", the significant loss of tribal identities, languages, and cultural traditions, even while he spoke out and advocated for a return to more "traditional Indian" values. He was known to say that one day there may well be no Native Americans, only "Native American Americans, like Polish Americans and Italian Americans." He wasn't alone in his view, and dozens of socially active tribal traditional people I know see the steady decline of the meaning of community traditions, cultures, and languages in the lives of their fellow tribesman as an important threat to the future identity of their communities as Native American. There appears to be evidence for the pessimistic view some hold.

Our marriage to non-Indians is at an all-time high, and Native Americans do so at the highest rate of any ethnicity in the U.S.; this even as the number of people who identity as Indians has grown, more than ten times as many in the 21st century as in 1890, the amount of those who are active in their tribal cultures and continue unique tribal traditions decreases, with one fifth as many as in 1890. That same year, a census conducted of the Indian Territory counted 18,636 people "of Negro descent in the Five Tribes" present in the Indian Territory, communities who were made fully members of the Five Tribes nearly four decades earlier by treaties negotiated in 1866 with their emancipation from bondage to the Cherokee, Creek, Choctaw, Chickasaw, and Seminole individuals who enslaved them. Today their descendants, like those emancipated captives a century and a half ago, are known as the Freedmen, and many are seeing their long historical ties to the Five Tribes being challenged once again.

Through several years of concern for the fate of the Freedmen, I was lucky enough to meet many people who were working hard to preserve their unique history and their present identities as members of the tribal communities of their ancestors and continue that legacy.

Individuals like Marilyn Vann, Ron Graham, and LeEtta Sampson would inspire me and others with their deeply held conviction that their family's histories as tribal members mattered, the passionate struggles they made to preserve those ancestral legacies for future generations, and their hopes for the betterment of their tribes as the nations they could be but were not as long as the shadow of racial discrimination was upon them, all inspired me to write on the matter. I owe a great thanks to these and many others who took time over the years to share their perspectives and concerns, fears and hopes, as the Freedmen people continue to navigate in what is at times still a very hostile corner of Indian Country in the small towns of eastern Oklahoma. The leadership and passionate service that Marilyn Vann has displayed through the years of seeking justice has been unequaled and her commitment to her community and tribe exemplary from my perspective.

The Freedmen of the Cherokee Nation and their forebears have long been among the communities of this largest of tribes, though their ancestors were held in bondage for generations before the American Civil War and slavery ripped apart the Cherokee, as it did America. They spoke the Cherokee language in most cases and labored to survive among the Cherokee people before and after the removal from the south to the Indian Territory, as in the hard years after their emancipation in the wake of the Civil War. They participated in the unique way of life found among the Five Tribes during the late 1800's and 1900's, but they are today asking themselves hard questions as to the meaning of their identity as part of the Cherokee Nation of Oklahoma, and how fierce a social and legal fight is worth it to maintain that connection. Their legitimacy as Cherokee people being questioned is nothing new for them as being on the margins of both native and American society is a situation the Freedmen of the Five Tribes have long endured. As the descendants of persons with African ancestry among the Five Tribes and enslaved for the enrichment of others, such a challenging legacy still resounds in the lives of many to this day (Sturm, 2014).

At the heart of the Freedmen's struggle lies a legal, political, and social balancing act. As Americans individual tribal members have specific rights well known to any citizen. That tribes have an inherent right to self-governance is at the foundation of their constitutionally established status, and that inherent power reserved and intentionally exercised is not delegated by congressional acts, though Congress can limit tribal sovereignty. Unless a treaty or federal statute removes a power, however, the tribe is assumed to still possess it. Current federal policy in the United States recognizes this sovereignty and the government-to-government relations between Washington, D.C. and the over 567 federally recognized American Indian tribes, and long has with the exception of a few episodes in the historical relationship. The fine balance of tribe's sovereign right to determine their members and individual tribal member's rights as Americans lies at the heart of the Freedmen's struggle.

The fate of the Freedmen of the Five Tribes in Oklahoma is important because their inclusion by treaty rests on the bedrock of the status of the Native American identity and sovereignty. Yet the racialized view of the Native American identity would obscure this long standing reality of tribal status being founded on nationhood not race. With tribes determining their own members, there are many tribes who have long lost the appearance of identifiably Indian ancestry among many members. The Cherokee Nation, like several in northeastern Oklahoma, is one such tribe. The Cherokee had significant intermarriage with whites even before removal in the 1830's, and is such that the majority of the over 300,000 enrolled members have tiny fractions of Indian ancestry.

A treaty in 1866 negotiated between the Cherokee Nation and the U.S. federal government in the days after the Civil War conveyed to the freed slaves in the nation no longer held by individual Cherokee tribal member's full tribal citizenship (Treaty with the Cherokee, 1866, 14 Stat. 799). Court cases since then have documented struggles by Cherokee Freedmen in Oklahoma to fully secure that asserted full tribal citizenship within the Cherokee Nation, their legal and ethical right by treaty many say. The inclusion they hope for has been challenged for many reasons. Because the Cherokee Nation does not determine tribal membership on the basis of blood quantum, arguably a more obviously racialized marker of group inclusion, as many tribes across the country do, but instead on lineal descent and a genealogical based measure of belonging, the crossroads of race and sovereignty encountered in the struggle are all the more significant.

The Cherokee were not the only tribe wrestling with the Freedmen's identity in the last few decades. In 2000, the Seminole Nation held a referendum for a constitutional amendment establishing new membership rule requiring that members had to have one-eighth blood quantum, of documented descent from an Indian by blood tribal member recorded on the Dawes Rolls, a development which would expel many of the historically associated "black Seminole", and the General Council prohibited representatives from the two Freedmen Bands from participating in the vote. With the change, about 1,200 Freedmen were excluded from tribal membership and most benefits afforded to the tribe. While differing in some ways from the other Five Tribes in their relationship with the African descendants among them, the modern Seminole Nation of Oklahoma is today less welcoming in its dealings with Black Seminole than when the two peoples fought for their freedom as one in the Florida swamps a century and a half ago. Though the Freedmen remained part of the tribe, albeit with less benefits, the scars remain for some raw and painful.

For the Cherokee Freedmen and their struggle, 2017 would find the U.S. District Court deciding for the Freedmen descendants and the U.S. Department of the Interior in the Cherokee Nation v. Raymond Nash et al. and Marilyn Vann et al. cases. The ruling clarified that according to Article 9 of the Cherokee Treaty of 1866, the Cherokee Freedmen descendants indeed have present rights to citizenship in the Cherokee Nation, which are coextensive with the rights of those Cherokee "by blood", a decision arrived at after sustained and painful struggle among the Cherokee, which saw accusations of racism, intolerance, and maleficence thrown about. The Creek Nation as well was witness to efforts for justice by its historic Freedmen people, which has led some to decide to seek acknowledgement as a separate tribe. The Freedmen from all tribes have through the organization headed by Marilyn Vann, called the Descendants of Freedmen of the Five Civilized Tribes, become more aware, more involved and more heard in their growing efforts at preserving their unique heritage, and in defending their identity as parties to the Treaty of 1866 and as people of Indian Country.

Native American status, like that of racial identity in the 21st century in America, is an evolving and dynamic topic that for the average person is full of unanswered questions, social pitfalls, legal exceptions, and erroneous assumptions. From the increasing presence of persons self-identified as Indian[1] on the constitutionally mandated federal census, to expanding challenges to the viability of tribal communities often located in sparsely populated regions and surviving on diminishing funding, leads to questioning of the sustainability of past

---

[1] University of Kansas sociologist Joane Nagel posits the tripling in the amount of Americans self-reporting American Indian as their race in the U.S. Census from 1960 to 1990, increasing from 523,591 to 1,878,285, to federal Indian policy, American ethnic politics, and American Indian political activism.

paradigms of indigenous identity going forward. In more ways than one the modern Native American community is stretching thinner and thinner, biologically and financially, even as Native American culture and traditions are celebrated more than ever.

Russell Means, longtime leader of the American Indian Movement said in the 1970's that "We might speak our language, we might look like Indians and sound like Indians, but we won't be Indians. (Peroff, 1997)", which may lead one to ask what are the factors driving Native American identity formation and destruction today. The tension between social and legal forces at work both within "Indian Country' and from external mainstream populations is increasing as endogamy within indigenous community's decrease and legal, economic, and social stakes for genuine tribal-based identities rise. Alarmingly, endangered languages, cultural survival, and ideas of peoplehood are the poker chips in a game of identity survival that has social, legal, and biological dimensions.

Racialized definitions of native identity are being increasingly asserted by those within and outside of the Native American community even as out marriage to non-Indians is higher than that of any other ethnicity in the country. Native America is transitioning, but to what? The struggle to define just what is "Native American" or who is an "American Indian" for those who consider themselves to be Native American, as well as for people who do not, is fiercer than ever and daily unfolds in homes, tribal councils, and court rooms all over this country and even beyond.

A widely accepted definition of identity that will provide for a functional legal, social, and personal purpose is hard to arrive at in a diverse democratic society such as that of modern America. There are different markers which have been employed to define individual and group degrees of "Indianness" across time and place, as the quoted words of Russell Means, Wilma Mankiller, and Scott Momaday in the front of the book illustrate. Importantly the source and purpose of the intended use of the definition have a significant role in what definition is used; characterizations of "Indianness" including cultural, social, genetic, legal, and self-identity are most frequently invoked (Parades, 1995).

Should the definition of what constitutes a "Native American" be changeable across time and situation, is it more a dynamic social synthesis frequently shifting, or is it more accurate to define "Indianness" in a static way with ties firmly bound to past meanings? Definitions posited by some may be founded in approaches Indians themselves use to adapt to the dominant social mainstream, an oppositional process by which the separations between Indians and the dominant groups are maintained intentionally. This process by which the ethnic identity of any group is developed and renewed as social organizations and cultures evolve is ongoing, relational, and multifaceted.

Identity in Native American communities and the reserved right to determine their own tribal membership has been a subject of contentious debate since the start of the federal-tribal relationship. In securing federal recognition, American Indians unlike any other ethnic group, must continually prove their identity. Such an unrelenting challenge in some cases forces tribal communities to accept whatever indigenous histories or social postures necessary to assure their own members and others of the legitimate Native American identity.

Political realties and uncertainty of funding and status for Native American tribes today as in the past, again brings forth pressing questions of identity and individual and tribal self-determination into the dialogue of Indian Country. What are the most appropriate venues to recognize and define clearly what and who is an Indian? To what degree is it necessary for governmental officials and tribes to frequently reconstruct operational definitions to accommodate the current sociopolitical realities of American Indian identity? Such questions have need to be addressed in consideration of the present state of collective American Indian identity politics and their impacts on individual Americans.

Long an observer of the struggles of southeastern Indian tribes and the many mixed race "American Isolate" communities of the east, nearly 2 decades of life in Oklahoma has rewarded me with relationships, participation, and experiences among dozens of tribal communities that are wholly rewarding and deeply treasured, and revelatory of these impacts of identity politics on the individual. Given many of my examples and perspectives are drawn from and shaped by public records and news media sources, my interpretation of the issues addressed are informed as well by several years of formal and informal research and fieldwork in several Native American communities that took place between 1996 when I first moved to Oklahoma and 2010 when I graduated from Rogers State University with an undergraduate degree in Sociology, one earned in Claremore in the Cherokee Nation and immersed in its people and history. During the period addressed, I had close relationships with community members and political leaders both in the Cherokee Indian community and among the Descendants of the Freedmen of the Five Civilized Tribes Association, as well as with other relevant organizations.

During the years I spent monitoring the story of the Freedmen's struggle and living in the Cherokee Nation, most people I met in Oklahoma claimed Indian heritage and had the notion that the Indian blood that courses through their veins, of any quantum or degree, is an inheritance of a type, and their narratives they shared communicated to me that their ancestry reflected a somewhat bifurcated identity, similar to my own as a "Florida Dominicker". To have "Indian blood" is to hold an authentic connection to the land that predates statehood and speaks to a common past that is at the core of Oklahoma Indian identity; dozens of tribes were all brought from far away homelands and most tribal members today have a comingling of tribal ancestries regardless of the tribe they are an enrolled member of.

A good example of this is my daughter-in-law, who is half Cheyenne-Arapaho (the tribe with whom she is enrolled), a quarter Sac and Fox and a quarter Shawnee. She is full blood Indian but of different tribal lineages. This is Oklahoma and is Indian Country today, where of the more than three dozen federally recognized tribes[2], there are those tribes who have few if any enrolled members who appear "identifiably Indian", living alongside those who have many full blood members still. Most are somewhere in between.

Because the United States Supreme Court has held repeatedly that "American Indian" is not a racial classification under the law but is rather a political classification, referring to citizenship in the "domestic, dependent nations" that entered into many treaties with the United States, issues relating to the identity of those in "Indian Country" is among the most complex found anywhere in what is arguable among one of the most diverse countries on earth. As I and other observers watched during the years of the "Freedmen controversy", it was sometimes presented as a case of the mostly "white Cherokee" of the Cherokee Nation was determined to drive out "black Cherokee", dis-enrolling individuals and expelling families long part of the Oklahoma Indian communities where they had lived for generations.

The Trump era has opened up new vistas in the critique of Indian Country in some corners but the stirrings of

---

[2] These the surviving remnant of nearly 100 tribal groups brought to Indian Territory over a century.

the recent conservative victory can be found in public reactions to the internal struggle of the Cherokee over the Freedmen's status. The always vigilant critics of Native American sovereignty wanting to show that all Indians programs that advantage Indian people are but a fig leaf for racial discrimination against non-Indians and ought to be prohibited by the 14th Amendment for denial of equal protection of the law sensed in the litigation and social upheaval an opportunity to strike a blow at Indian sovereignty.

The Cherokee Nation, and no less so the Creek and Seminole, in seeking to expel the Freedmen, gave fuel to a growing political movement serving the interests of whites asserting reverse discrimination. Caught at the intersection of the short-sighted interests of some in leadership of the Cherokee Nation in making Cherokee citizenship an issue of race, (with "white" Cherokee in and "black" Cherokee out) and the victory of the established paradigm of the true 'nation within a nation' model reinforced in the Freedman cases ultimate resolution, the Cherokee now must once again reconcile their past identity with that of future generations. Since the Cherokee Nation does not determine tribal membership on the basis of blood quantum as many tribes across the country do, but instead on lineal descent, the realities revealed at the crossroads of identity, race, and sovereignty encountered in their struggle for inclusion and authenticity are all the more significant.

In the early 20th century, the Creek, Seminole, Choctaw and Cherokee Nations were enumerated in the headlong drive to Oklahoma statehood that included the disillusionment of the many tribal governments of Indian territory, listing those included, on the Freedmen and "by Blood" parts of The Dawes Rolls alike. The closing of that century and the start of the 21st would find all four tribes seeking or having disenfranchised the descendants of Freedmen of the ability to exercise their rights as citizens.

When questioned about these developments, tribal politicians forwarded the opinion that "these people" were listed as Freedmen, not Indians by blood, and so are "not really part of the tribe"[3]. But there were several problems with this response. First and importantly, it ignored that the Freedmen Rolls when they were created in the 19th century relied in part on the "one-drop rule", the social experience of the non-Indian registrars of the Dawes Rolls, a view of race and identity somewhat different from the long intermixed identities of Indian Territory residents by far. Enshrined in the 1896 ruling in Plessy v. Ferguson, the one-drop rule meant that people of mixed-race descent could legally still be considered solely black. This effectively erased the Native ancestry of most people on the Freedmen Roll; indeed, even if they and their ancestors had possessed Native ancestry, there was no official record of it. That quandary would haunt their descendants.

---

[3] Oral history interview Owasso Oklahoma 2004

The Cherokee Nation was forced to free their enslaved population in 1863, and after the Civil War, the other tribes did the same, with all but the Chickasaw eventually granting Freedmen full citizenship in the tribal community as the treaty of 1866 mandated. When the U.S. Congress established the Dawes Commission charged with dissolving collective tribal lands and allotting parcels to individual tribal members, many thousands of Freedmen came before the commission to prove their tribal membership and their right to a share of land, which for the most part they received. The granting of that allotment by inclusion on a role as Freedmen or Indian by blood would unwittingly create a legacy of disputation and for some alienation from the Cherokee community of those generations down the line. So what has changed in the century since the Dawes Roll?

For one the awareness of the complexity of identity in modern America. Another is a much better understanding of the high degree of subjective judgement and ignorance of the complex social realities by those compiling records that have long been used to establish tribal membership. The Dawes Commission was established in 1893 to enforce the General Allotment Act of 1887 also known as the Dawes Act. It was charged with cajoling tribes to cede their land to the United States and divide what remained into individual allotments. The Dawes commission required Native Americans to claim citizenship in only one tribe and register as such on the Dawes Rolls, a record meant to be a definitive record of individuals with Indian blood.

The Curtis Act was passed in 1898, and was focused on the "Five Tribes" of the Cherokee, Choctaw, Chickasaw, Creek and Seminole Nations in Indian Territory. This Act was aimed at forcing them to accept their individual land allotments by registering on the Dawes Rolls.

The Commission registrars erected tents in Indian Territory and set about enrolling people, Bill Welge, director emeritus of the Oklahoma Historical Society's Office of American Indian Culture and Preservation said in an interview[4]. In this rough and tumble setting registrars poured over written records, recorded oral history testimonials and created enrollment documents for those judged to have qualifications met for inclusion on the roll. Those enrollees included authentic Indians and citizens of the Five Tribes such as the Freedmen and "intermarried whites", but included lots of people with questionable heritage or ties to the tribes as well. Graft and backdoor dealings proliferated.

> *"Commissioners took advantage of their positions and enrolled people who had very minimal or questionable connections to the tribes, they were not averse to taking money under the table."*

These were documented cases of the fraud and double dealing occurring during the Dawes commissions duty to execute its responsibility of allotment, already

---

[4] https://indiancountrymedianetwork.com/history/people/paying-play-indian-dawes-rolls-legacy-5-indians/

underhanded in the light of modern 21st century understandings of governmental responsibilities to indigenous peoples, made ore so by graft and corruption. The repercussions of such shady dealings over a century ago are enormous now in the lives of those entangled in the vagaries of the identity politics of modern Indian Country.

> *"Now we have people who are white but who can trace their names back to the rolls used by tribal nations to ascertain who has rights as citizens…that means we have white people who have the ability to vote at large; it means political rights; it means the potential to influence tribal policy on a whole range of issues; it means people have access to health care, education and employment. The implications are quite profound for people who got away with fraud."*

To make the Dawes enrollment even more complicated, even as non-Natives "paid to play Indian", there were countless authentic Indians whose did trust of the government ran deep and who chose not to register with the Dawes Rolls at all relates Gene Norris, a genealogist at the Cherokee National Historical Society. That meant those with legitimate claims to tribal enrollment and the benefits it extended were now excluded. The Cherokee Keetoowah Nighthawks and the Crazy Snake movement among the Creek Nation's traditionalist both would see individuals resisting allotment and the violation of the treaties between their tribes and the federal governmental that the Indians had negotiated and put faith in.

Holdouts among the Cherokee that resisted allotment often belonged to several societies in the Cherokee Nation mostly composed of full bloods. Led by Redbird Smith, the Keetoowah Nighthawk movement was very vocal in the refusing to enroll or accept the allotment from the Dawes Commission. The pressure was relentless and Smith and other leaders was arrested in 1902 and forced to accept enrollment. Ultimately some 5000 or so Cherokee and other traditional people continued several more years to resist enrollment, but they were unsuccessful for the most part, as in time they were enrolled without their consent and finally allotted land and money as the Cherokee Nation was forcibly politically dismantled (Bailey, 1996). Norris relates the degree of chaos involved with the Dawes enrollment.

> *"Native Americans are the only racial group defined by blood, even that was arbitrary. In the 1890s, siblings who talked to different commissioners emerged with different blood quantum. Because they didn't apply together, some of them have different blood degrees."*

The Dawes Rolls would alter ever after the means the federal government used to define citizenship in

Oklahoma and in many ways establish the methods in which the tribes still use to define themselves.

"In 1900, one woman registered on the rolls with 1/256 Cherokee blood", Norris relates, a number unsurprising when one peruses the blood quanta of contemporary Cherokee Nation citizens. Amazingly there are in the 21st century, enrolled members of the Cherokee Nation whom have as little as 1/8,196 Indian blood[5]. The Dawes Rolls then and now is a "very inaccurate" gauge of Indian citizenship, Norris said. This and similar observations though have hardly been part of decades of dialogue about the challenges to modern tribal enrollment among the Five Tribes in Oklahoma.

Sovereignty implies that Native Americans as "dependent nations" are not minorities, but more so it is a political status unlike any other in the country. Mindful of the continuing discussion on tribal sovereignty revealed by the Freedmen's struggle for inclusion and the role of race and sovereignty in Indian Country, American Indian as a political status is at times ignored as the tropes of race based identity politics are forwarded even as calls for social equality and inclusion grow louder on the social and political scene. Certainly the reconciliation of the two poles of tribal sovereignty and individual civil rights of tribal members must by nature be an ongoing discussion to keep pace with the swiftly shifting social and political terrain tribes'

---

[5] https://indiancountrymedianetwork.com/history/people/paying-play-indian-dawes-rolls-legacy-5-indians/

today traverse in an era when the authenticity of the Native American identity is more questioned than ever.

All indigenous peoples have an increased visibility in the last 50 years because of efforts from within their own communities and organizations in part. However, refining the legal instruments that guarantee the autonomy, cultural integrity, protection of their special needs as dependent domestic nations has not been easy. Native peoples are the inheritors of an important American legacy and practitioners of unique cultures and ways of relating to other people and to the environment.

Indian communities have retained many social, cultural, economic and political characteristics that are distinct from those of the dominant American society in which they live. Their cultural differences notwithstanding, the various Native American nations around the United States share common problems related to the protection of their rights as distinct peoples. Few outside of legal and academic circles are aware that federal constitutional constraints on governmental action established in the Bill of Rights and the Fourteenth Amendment do not apply to, or constrain, tribal government; indeed, the primary source for individual rights to constrain tribal government authority is tribal law. The Indian Civil Rights Act (ICRA), a part of the 1968 Civil Rights Act, is the source for individual rights and tribal government actions in their roles as modern governments.

This act extends most of the constitutional protections of the federal Bill of Rights to individuals under the jurisdiction of Indian tribal governments and for the most part those guaranteed protections are enforceable exclusively in tribal courts and governmental venues. To preserve specific functions of tribal governance and sovereignty, portions of the Bill of Rights were modified or left out. the methods recommended in 1969 have been followed by tribal courts, most having generally interpreted the provisions of the ICRA like that of the leading commentary on the Act: "Unless the record shows a willingness to modify tribal life wherever necessary to impose ordinary constitutional standards, courts should take this legislation as a mandate to interpret statutory standards within the framework of tribal life."

Complicating the function of law in Indian Country and playing a significant role in the case of the Freedmen is that Native American "governance" is not government in the western sense of authority and control. Native American systems of governance are more oft meaning more like leadership over a community, and additionally it is problematic to describe Native American "government" in a definite manner due to the fact that there are many different indigenous tribes with different forms of governing. Ancient traditions inform and influence even the most cutting edge tribal councils and Indian corporate endeavors today. The imprint of the communal past and collective decision making traditions can be found in countless modern tribal constitutions and bylaws.

For indigenous communities worldwide, relinquishing rights to self-government in favor of status as an ethnic group among many others is an important contemporary issue. The loss of their existence as a nation or self-governing people for an ethnic group status is an unappealing compromise, one which most Native Americans would be unwilling to make since the countless ethnic groups in the U.S. do not have rights to self-government that precede the formation of the Constitution and America. The relationship of the land, ancient tribal religion, modern self-government and community identity are closely interrelated and differ significantly from the mainstream American law and custom.

The culture of most tribes are founded on self-government as indigenous communities, though takes forms that are significantly different from those of many contemporary nation-state governments. But whatever form of governance a tribe has contemporarily, it like all must be accountable for its actions to and for its citizens. The decision by some Cherokee individuals to establish chattel slavery among a people to whom it was unknown resounded across generations; "The truth is that the practice of slavery will forever cast a shadow on the great Cherokee Nation" said Principal Chief Wilma Mankiller, and it was true.

The crossroads of identity that the Cherokee Nation found itself at in the playing out of the Freedmen's status as Cherokee citizens is one that, like the preceding decision of the Cherokee Nation v. Georgia, 30 U.S. (5

Pet.) 1 (1831), is at the heart of the matter of Native American identity and the future of tribal communities in the great American experiment. That long ago case, wherein the Cherokee Nation sought a federal injunction against laws passed by the state of Georgia seeking to deprive Cherokee of rights within its boundaries, and the Supreme Court not hearing the case on its merits but instead ruling that it had no original jurisdiction in the matter, (as the Cherokees were a dependent nation, with a relationship to the United States like that of a "ward to its guardian,") shaped the lives of generations of Native Americans afterwards. The decision in

The headlines in late 2017 that the two parties of Cherokee people involved in the decade's long struggle were "linking arms (and) marching forward" meant that while one chapter closed another began in the ongoing narrative of belonging and identity in Indian country. Cherokee Nation's acceptance of the ruling on Freedmen citizenship was part of this important and continuous dialogue between its people, and the Cherokee Nation. As Marilyn Vann put it *"We've gone quite a bit ways in the last few years but we got a ways to go."* Looking in deeper detail at the struggles by the Freedmen of the Five Tribes can help observers to understand what's to come as the role of Indian Country in the American experiment continues to be debated and the place of mainstream American culture and identity is subjected to the same in Indian Country. An experience ongoing since contact, the crossroads of identity that Indian Country again finds itself at in the

21st century is one inclusive of complex and shifting issues of individual and tribal sovereignty and historical affiliation.

Contents

INTRODUCTION i
Contents xxvi
THREE RACES, TWO CHOICES, ONE HISTORY 1
CHEROKEE 19
CREEK 39
SEMINOLE 55
DISENROLLMENT 93
CONCLUSION 101
Index 109

THREE RACES, TWO CHOICES, ONE HISTORY

The Indians, whites, and persons of African ancestry resident in the Indian Territory were faced with a choice like the rest of the communities of the continent who were holding slaves, as the likelihood of war on the horizon became a reality. by fighting to preserve that peculiar institution and striking new treaties with the confederates, or by choosing loyalty to the Union and fleeing north to Kansas, all involved would contribute to the history of the Cherokee Nation, the Indian Territory, and the United States. The others of the Five Tribes were much like the Cherokee in the steady increase in slaveholding in the Indian Territory since their arrival in their new home in the west. But the tradition of holding others in bondage had long roots.

Slavery was no stranger among the American Indians of the centuries past; the Cherokee first encountered the institution of chattel slavery when tribal members were enslaved by English colonists but, like most Native Americans, the Indians put into bondage quickly showed themselves to be more trouble than they were worth and enslavement of indigenous peoples was found to expensive and difficult to become reliably instituted. So there was the importation of those who could be made to work.

Slave holding was a part of indigenous communities in the Americas long before the arrival of enslaved Africans and their European captors on the North American scene though. the advent of European colonialism and the subsequent establishment of the widespread use of enslaved persons in America meant that American Indians found themselves soon fighting for survival in a global economy in part resting on a racialized system reliant on the trafficking for profit of people. "Slavery was not peculiar to indigenous societies," where captives were prisoners of war obtained from enemy tribes, Christina Snyder states in her book **Slavery in Indian Country: The Changing Face of Captivity in Early America**, but *"the form that slavery took in the antebellum South and elsewhere in the colonial Americas,"* was new.

The Five Tribes[6] of the Cherokee, Creek, Seminole, Chickasaw, and Choctaw whose original homeland was located in the southeastern interior, like their white neighbors saw the increasing presence of racialized chattel slavery in the late 18th century among an increasingly wealthy and politically active mixed blood elite. White Southerners encouraged the tribes to take part in the enslavement of blacks as an aspect of the American Federal Government's "civilization" of the Indians policy. In ***The Westo Indians: Slave Traders of the Early Colonial South***, Erin E. Browne relates the strategy the Westo tribe used to gain access to guns, ammunition, metal tools and other goods.

They would capture tribal adversaries to barter to the English Virginians, and they appear to have been successful at their profession, that is until war broke out between the Carolina colony and the Westo in 1679. The colonials destroyed the Westo in 1680, and the neighboring Savannah Shawnee people moved into their lands and assumed for themselves the role as the chief Indian trading partner with the Carolina colony. Ironically the fate of the surviving Westo was most likely enslavement and shipment to work on sugarcane plantations in the West Indies.

Initially in the colonial era, there would be thousands of Native Americans enslaved in Colonial New England, according to some researchers. Alan Gallay states that between 1670 and 1715, Indians were exported into slavery in greater numbers through Charleston, South Carolina than Africans were imported. One scholar who made a summation of the total population of enslaved people, forwards that as many as 2 million or more indigenous people in the Americas may have been enslaved over the centuries that it existed.

In ***Bonds of Alliance: Indigenous and Atlantic Slaveries in New France***, Brett Rushforth writes of the main difference in the

---

[6] The term used in this work is the "Five Tribes"; previously the "Five Civilized Tribes" was used, and derives from the colonial and early federal period in the history of the United States. It refers to five Native American nations—the Cherokee, Chickasaw, Choctaw, Creek (Muscogee), and Seminole. The latter term has been criticized for its ethnocentric definition of civilization, and will not be used in this work.

THREE RACES, TWO CHOICES, ONE HISTORY

indigenous forms of bondage and that of the chattel slavery of the European colonist that soon would be taken up by some tribes.

> *"Rather than a closed slave system designed to move slaves 'up and out'—excluding slaves and their descendants from full participation in their masters' society, even when freed—indigenous slavery moved captives 'up and in' toward full, if forced, assimilation."*

In the South the exponential growth of agriculture meant that the initial demand for Indian slaves influenced and in many regions seriously disrupted the political and social connections between tribes. With an incentive to raid for slaves, tribe's posture towards one another became increasingly aggressive and violence on their borders increased.

> *"Once Europeans showed up and they demanded that the supply of Native slaves' amp up to meet the demand, Native practices regarding slaves changed, so people who might once have been adopted or killed now became slaves."*

Those captured in war, taken during slave raids, or purchased from third parties and enslaved in the 1600's by Europeans would have a fate somewhat different than the enslavement experienced by those enslaved by other Indian tribes; made captive by another tribe, an Indian would be subject to community traditions that established the features of his or her treatment while held.

But after an Indian tribe sold a captured Indian to Europeans, the captive was subsumed into a global system of bondage and was now a commodity on an international marketplace hungry for free labor. The humanity now reduced to a commodified measure of labor, and pushed along in a wide ranging network of exchange, the indigenous enslaved person could be sold very far away. Rushforth states cases of Apaches and other Plains peoples being sold, through Quebec, to the Caribbean. The legislation of human bondage in the colonies was one more area of economic venture for them. Virginia General Assembly defined some terms of slavery in 1705, inclusive of Indians.

The Freedmen's Quandary

> *"All servants imported and brought into the Country ... who were not Christians in their native Country ... shall be accounted and be slaves. All Negro, mulatto and Indian slaves within this dominion ... shall be held to be real estate. If any slave resists his master ... correcting such slave, and shall happen to be killed in such correction ... the master shall be free of all punishment ... as if such accident never happened.[7]"*

Along with the adoption of other European goods and practices by members of the Cherokee Nation, came slavery. More than any other tribe, the Cherokee Nation would count more enslaved people within its boundaries and the establishment of chattel enslavement was a mark on the Cherokee Nation's and the other southeastern tribe's histories, as it is the United States. Unsurprisingly this adoption of human bondage for profit would be established among the Indian nations primarily from the efforts of the mixed blood gentry of the southeastern tribes to amass personal wealth, something antithetical to the native egalitarianism of tribal lifeways. The slavery episode of southeastern Indian history would set into motion actions which resound across the generations to this day.

Some who witnessed the years of commitment at the dawn of the 21st century by the Cherokee Freedmen and their advocates to secure their status as tribal citizens would say that after the last several decades of social and legal struggle, the tribes who practiced slavery and the descendants of those they held in bondage are still paying for the costs of the "peculiar institution" even unto a century and a half later. When slavery took root in the old south, it spread quickly. The Cherokee Nation exceeded their peers in the adoption of the white southern slave culture and as a tribe they profited the most from their enslavement of fellow human beings, with some sources citing that by 1809 there were 600 enslaved persons living in the Cherokee Nation and that by 1835 the number had increased to 1,600.

---

[7] The Terrible Transformation: From Indentured Servitude to Racial Slavery". PBS. 2009. Retrieved 03/07/2018.

THREE RACES, TWO CHOICES, ONE HISTORY

Investigation of the "slave schedule" tied to the 1860 Federal Census reveals that members of the Cherokee Nation owned almost as many enslaved persons as all the rest of the Five Tribes combined, totaling nearly 4,600. In order of magnitude of numbers of enslaved people enumerated among the Five Tribes of the Indian Territory were the Choctaw Nation with 2,344, the Creek Nation with 1,532 (a tribe with a history of slaveholding very similar to that of the Cherokee; it would see its own enslaved people's descendants asserting their ties to the collective national tribal identity due to the legacy of slavery and the 1866 treaty freeing them and making their descendants tribal citizens). Today all those past enslaved persons have tens of thousands of descendants across the country, a people still known today as "Freedmen", like their ancestors.

Of the Five Tribes removed to Indian Territory, only the Seminole Nation never adopted chattel slavery, per se. While still in the southeast, many escaped enslaved persons of African ancestry would make it to the Seminole frontier in Florida, where they took refuge in the Indian tribal communities. These refugees were treated as subject peoples, but nobody owned them as they did with the Creek or Cherokee. The Seminole Nation was the sole government of the Five Tribes relocated to Indian Territory that never legislated slave codes. These laws where they were instituted were "punitive regulations of human property directed to maintaining the peculiar institution in law and custom and enforceable at the whim of any free person"[8].

African people who escaped bondage and established themselves in Seminole tribal territory lived in their own separate but nearby communities, many carried firearms, and their families were liable for taxation on a portion of their crops by Seminole communities to which they were attached; for the most part this was the norm of the bondage experienced by blacks among the Seminole Indians, the cultural conservatism that ran through their culture and the tribal adherence to it keeping the most egregious aspects of non-

---

[8] https://indiancountrymedianetwork.com/news/politics/disappearing-indians-part-ii-the-hypocrisy-of-race-in-deciding-whos-enrolled/

Indian culture at a distance in some measure. These "black Seminole" who took up homes in the Florida wilderness were seen as allies and were expected to provide warriors and support for the frequent and repeated wars with the European colonists, and later the subsequent involvement of the United States when it inherited the hopes of conquering the tribe still known today as "the Unconquered".

"Spanish Florida" was a refuge for those fleeing enslavement for at least 70 years, when the American Revolution brought the new United States onto the scene, and eventually into possession of Florida and conflict with the Seminole. Communities of Black Seminoles were well established in the region, with settlements attached to the major Seminole Indian towns. The era during the Revolutionary War would see the Seminole make alliance with the British. During this time Blacks and Indians in the Seminole settlements came into increased contact with each other, and though the Seminole held some as slaves, it was as mentioned significantly different from that practiced by the Creek and other Southeast Indian tribes, and was uniquely a Seminole form of bondage.

Arrival of hostilities during the War of 1812 found black and Indian Seminole mostly sided with the British against the Americans, in a struggle in which they strengthened their internal social and cultural ties, connections which would last into the modern era for some. The frequent upheavals of the 20th century, from Dawes Allotment, to statehood, the Great Depression, tribal reorganization, then restoration of sovereign status and modern economic and political influences on tribal identities among the Five Tribes, have all led to a fraying of the historic ties between those of Indian and those of African ancestries.

Though many eastern tribes, and especially the Seminole, have long histories of contact during the colonial era and afterwards with African descended peoples, the social distance[9] between the

---

[9] Social distance is the perceived or desired degree of remoteness between a member of one social group and the members of another, as evidenced in the level of intimacy tolerated between them.

THREE RACES, TWO CHOICES, ONE HISTORY

two populations has increased during the late 20th century. Among the Creek, Seminole, and Cherokee Nations of Oklahoma, recent years would see controversies take center stage as persons of African descent amongst the historic populations associated with these tribes strived in many cases to assert both an African as well as Native American hybrid identity. In the historic Muscogee (Creek) Nation as in all those mentioned, "Freedmen" was a term for emancipated African descendants who were formerly enslaved by Creek Nation tribal members before 1866, and also for their descendants until today. Some had native ancestry in addition to African, and most had some degree of European admixture as well, DNA tests revealed.

During the Civil War, the politics of the Five Tribes were best described as splintered along assimilated versus traditional, and slave-holding mixed blood versus full blood lines, as the Choctaw and Chickasaw had factions who fought predominantly alongside the Confederates while the Creek and Seminole had some groups who similarly fought alongside the Union forces as well as Confederates. The Cherokee Nation would see triggered within the tribe an internal conflict between the majority Confederate sympathizers and the minority, who were pro-Union.

Factions within the Five Tribes that signed treaties with the confederates included the Creek Nation (July 10, 1861), the Choctaw and Chickasaw (July 12, 1861), the Seminole (August 1, 1861) and the Cherokee Nation (October 7, 1861). As well other tribes signed agreements with the Southern forces, including the Shawnees, Delaware, Wichita and affiliated tribes then residing on "leased territories" within the western part of Choctaw and Chickasaw territories (August 12, 1861). Small factions among the Comanche, Osage, Quapaw and Seneca as well submitted their signatures in 1861.

The persons enslaved and held by affluent and more assimilated "mixed blood" Creeks, many who fought for the Confederacy, were emancipated under the Creek Nation's 1866 treaty with the victorious federal authorities of the United States following the American Civil War. The treaties negotiated with the "Five

Tribes"[10] after the war, just like the Dawes enrollment process, would play a large part in the fate of the emancipated Freedman's descendants a century later and their struggle for inclusion in the tribe.

During the Civil War conflicts in which some factions of the Creek Nation in Indian Territory had allied with the Confederacy, the American federal government found its staunchest supporters among the often full blood and traditional Indians, who were driven north out of Indian Territory to Kansas where they suffered greatly during the war years. Sadly, after its end the American federal government chose to punish the Creek Nation as an entire tribe for the Confederate sympathizer's actions, taking retribution against the nation as a whole and confiscating tribally held lands as a result.

On Feb. 19, 1863 the Cherokee Nation issued "An Act Providing for the Abolition of Slavery in the Cherokee Nation". This decree called for "the immediate emancipation of all Slaves in the Cherokee Nation." In a treaty ratified on July 27, 1866, the Cherokee Nation, much like the other Five Tribes declared that the newly emancipated Freedmen "and their descendants, shall have all the rights of native Cherokees." Similar acts tool place among the Creek, Choctaw, and Chickasaw as well. During Reconstruction after the Civil War, new Reconstruction Treaties were signed with the several nations in Indian Territory that had entered into treaties with the Confederate States of America. With the federal government setting forth new Reconstruction Treaties, many of these punished the tribes for their confederate sympathizers.

In light of these new agreements forged after the conflict, newly emancipated Creek and other tribal Freedmen who wished to stay in the Creek Nation in Indian Territory and in many cases having

---

[10] The term used in this work is the "Five Tribes"; previously the "Five Civilized Tribes" was used, and derives from the colonial and early federal period in the history of the United States. It refers to five Native American nations—the Cherokee, Chickasaw, Choctaw, Creek (Muscogee), and Seminole. The latter term has been criticized for its ethnocentric definition of civilization, and will not be used in this work.

THREE RACES, TWO CHOICES, ONE HISTORY

blood relatives among the Creek Indians, were to be granted full citizenship in the Creek Nation. The presence of people of African descent was not new among the tribes of the southeast. There had been many of the African descended slaves who generations before had removed with the Creeks from the Southeast in the 1830s, and they had lived and intermarried to some degree with the Indians since. Most Freedmen of any of the Five Tribes had worked the land since the removal era and coming to Indian Territory.

The complexity of the Freedmen identity is far beyond the oral history of Native American ancestry that oft heard in many African-American families; Indeed, geneticists have found the numbers of black Native Americans to be relatively small. When activist and scholar Henry Louis Gates looked into the subject, he found that only 5 percent of African-American people carry more than 2 percent Native American ancestry.

The "Freedman" title also is today inclusive of the modern descendants of those Civil War Era Freedman of Indian Territory, now found across the United States, but still concentrated in eastern Oklahoma. Most Cherokee Freedmen have predominantly African and African American lineage, but there is a minority who also have Cherokee ancestry, and can usually document it using pre-Dawes Rolls and collateral archival records. The actual number of Cherokee Freedmen with Indian ancestry is a debatable matter, with estimates ranging from one-tenth to one-third forwarded by some researchers (Cooper, 2011). In the time of the Civil War and since, there were Freedmen of partial Cherokee, Creek, or Seminole Indian ancestry by blood, but the registration process of persons as classed in several types of tribal citizenship by the Dawes Commission in the late 1800's, ("Indian by blood", "intermarried whites", "Freedmen", etc.) oft failed to record Freedmen with such Indian ancestry, as white enumerators listed the physical presentation of the individual with little inquiry to mixed ancestry, which was frequent.

While it is true that generally Cherokee Freedmen lack a Certificate Degree of Indian Blood (CDIB) and are socially viewed by many Cherokee citizens ignorant of the realities of the Dawes Allotment process as to have no blood ties to the Cherokee Nation, yet for many Freedmen families this is simply not true, and genetic testing has revealed the native ancestry present in many. Yet in fact many Freedmen with Cherokee Indian ancestry cannot obtain a CDIB because they descend from mixed black and Indian Cherokee who were enumerated based solely on racial presentation recorded on the Dawes Rolls by non-Indian individuals unfamiliar with the significant amount of interracial mixture among all the races that had been going on among the Cherokee and other southeastern Indians for more than a hundred of years.

Uninformed individual registrars working on the Dawes commissions effort at making allotments had most African appearing individuals enumerated solely on the Freedmen rolls of the Cherokee Nation census, with little inquiry to mixed blood. These Freedmen records are most often today interpreted as the "Black" rolls, rather than the "Cherokee by Blood" rolls, and the people listed there in as solely black, despite DNA tests showing that many do have Native American forebears. To attempt to simplify such a political, fluid, and complex racial environment as the Cherokee Nation at the turn of the twentieth century into broad categories such as "Cherokee by blood" or "Freedmen" and think those are accurate is to fundamentally misunderstand the history of the Cherokee, or of the populations of the southeast and Indian Territory.

In those regions racial mixing among all residents had been occurring since the 1600's, unabated to this very day. To utilize such a record known to be so arbitrary as a basis for enrollment by a modern tribal people is to accept wholeheartedly the colonization of one's own political process, according to the view of several anti-colonial Native American activists I spoke to.

> *"The unsettling truth for America, no pun intended, is for Indians to reinstate just and workable practices relating to tribal membership and identity based on present realities that preserve indigenous languages, cultures, and communities, not perpetuate colonial*

THREE RACES, TWO CHOICES, ONE HISTORY

institutions, assimilative intentions, and non-indigenous approaches to collective tribal identities[11]"

The Dawes Act set in motion a long running problematic definition of identity for the people living in the Indian Territory. The enrollment process that documented the citizens of the nation's there eligible for land allotments involved the establishment of rolls including the Freedmen Roll and the "by blood" roll. These two rolls bestowed on the enrollee distinctly differing rights, with Freedmen given less land, 40 acres compared with 60 given to Indians. In the years after the Dawes Roll was compiled, the nation's eventually made lineal descent from an ancestor included on the Dawes Roll necessary for tribal citizenship, despite the shaping of it through preconceived concepts about race that influenced which portion of the roll a person wound up on. People enumerated on the "by blood" roll could have varying "degrees" of Indian and white ancestry and many did, while those who had any black and Indian ancestry were often automatically put onto or transferred later to the Freedmen Roll.

The Dawes Act of 1887, also called the General Allotment Act, was adopted by Congress to survey Native American communally held lands and divide it into allotments for individual citizens, of which by the 1866 treaty the Freedmen were. Teddy Roosevelt said that *"in my judgment the time has arrived when we should definitely make up our minds to recognize the Indian as an individual and not as a member of a tribe. The General Allotment Act is a mighty pulverizing engine to break up the tribal mass."* It was envisioned that Indian persons who accepted an allotment and lived independently from the tribal body could be given American citizenship. The Dawes Act was to have several manifestations, being amended in 1891, in 1898 by the Curtis Act, and again in 1906 by the Burke Act. During the decades that its force played out in Indian Country, the "Five Tribes" of Indian Territory lost 90 million acres of former communal lands, these holdings of the Creek, Seminole, Choctaw, Chickasaw, and Cherokee were sold to non-Natives.

---

[11] Oral history interview Fort Walton Beach, Florida 2004

Outside of the question of if an individual applicant was ultimately placed on the by blood or freedmen rolls, what was the general requirements or goals of the Dawes Roll being complied? The Dawes Commission was given applications for tribal membership that exceeded a quarter of a million applicants and would eventually enroll more than 101,000 of those. [2]The Tribal Membership Rolls were closed on 4th of March 1907, and subsequently was by an Act of Congress approved on the 26th of April in 1906 (34 Stat. 370)[12].

Who was intended to be included on the Dawes Roll? The Dawes Commission was tasked with enrolling onto the rolls those that met several criteria. These criteria were that the applicant must physically resided within the boundaries of that particular nation, that they were alive (though not necessarily present) at the time of the Commission's enrollment of them, and lastly were shown on either the 1896 or 1880 Census for that particular tribe that they be acknowledged by the tribe as being a citizen. Who was not eligible to be included? Whites married to an Indian, applicants unable to document that they were enrolled on either of the two previously mentioned rolls (recognized by that particular tribe as a citizen). Included as well was all that were listed on either the 1896 or 1880 Census (including Cherokee Old Settlers called Keetoowah today). As would occur to some, people did not need to apply for the Dawes Rolls in person, there are cases where allotments were assigned without the consent or cooperation of the person.

The Dawes Commission intended to compile rolls of the members of each tribe to grant them an allotment form the tribes communal held lands, with the excess being sold to settlers. The Dawes Commission usually employed the tribes own previous membership rolls as the baseline for enrolling. The registrars for the Dawes Commission were tasked with preparing a tribal citizenship roll for each tribe that was based on each one's own previously prepared citizenship rolls, so in part the commissions clerks were generally cross-checking for those found on that document. The non-Indian registrars employed took testimony

---

[12] an additional 312 persons were enrolled under an act approved 1. August. 1914.

THREE RACES, TWO CHOICES, ONE HISTORY

from individuals and families, many times appearing in person to validate that they were listed on previous tribal rolls. Once they did the applicants would be enrolled and the Commission would grant their allotment to them.

To be sure there were those that refused to enroll and asserted its illegality under the treaties signed with their ancestors. The Dawes Commission employed Cherokee to go out and locate people unwilling to come in and enroll. They crisscrossed each district and when the person's resistant to enrollment were found they determined if the person sought was still alive and those present in the household. The Dawes Commission would hopefully confirm the results of those employed to locate people resistant to enrollment. In 1906 the Dawes Commission registrars again canvased the Indian Territory, seeking minor children and enrolling them also. The Commissioners did their work of enrolling the willing as well as the unwilling thoroughly, even if they were not fully informed of the complexities of their task in dealing with the peoples of the Five Tribes and their actions of arbitrary placement of some with Indian blood onto the Freedmen rolls.

Many individual Indians who were less assimilated than fellow tribesman, often unfamiliar with private land ownership, would sometimes fall prey to land speculators and criminal elements who overran the Indian Territory during the process of the allotments. Tribal people across the many native communities caught in the process would suffer from the erosion and breakdown of the social fabric of the tribes. The Dawes Act per se did not initially apply to the territory of the Cherokee, Creek, Choctaw, Chickasaw, Seminole, Miami, and Peoria in Indian Territory or the Osage, Sac, and Fox, in the Oklahoma Territory. Certain provisions of the Dawes Act were later applied to the Wea, Peoria, Kaskaskia, Piankeshaw, and Western Miami tribes by act of 1889 (Debo, 1940).

Allotment of the lands of these tribes was mandated by the Act of 1891, which amplified the provisions of the Dawes Act, and caused immeasurable harm to Indian lives. FDR's administration adopted the Indian Reorganization Act in the 1930's, and "blood quantum" would become cemented into federal Indian policy as the yardstick by which the governmental agencies determined the degree of Native American identity and trust services was extended to its constituents.

Revelatory of the many failings of the blood quantum system and the Dawes Allotment process was Angie Debo's landmark work, ***And Still the Waters Run: The Betrayal of the Five Civilized Tribes*** (1940). This important work documented the assimilative and damaging mechanisms of the allotment policy of the Dawes Act, later determined to apply to the Five Tribes through the Dawes Commission and the Curtis Act of 1898. The conclusions that it was systematically mismanaged and utilized as a tool to remove the Native Americans from stewardship of the little lands they still possessed and gain access to the Indian's natural resources resounded clearly. In the words of historian Ellen Fitzpatrick, the revelations of the degree of harm the allotment process inflicted on native communities as documented by Debo in her work "*advanced a crushing analysis of the corruption, moral depravity, and criminal activity that underlay white administration and execution of the allotment policy*" (Fitzpatrick, 2004).

Early 1893 would be the last days that the dozens of tribal groups found in Indian Territory still had possession of millions of acres, lands communally held and utilized, with the Cherokee Nation the most populous and powerful tribe among them. U.S. Secretary of the Interior Hoke Smith forwarded on November 28, 1893 instructions to Dawes and the other commission members involved. The contents of that correspondence were not made public at the time. The intentions behind the actions of the commission are apparent in the instructions Smith wrote to Dawes.

> *"Success in your negotiations will mean the total abolition of the tribal autonomy of the Five Civilized Tribes and the wiping out the quasi-independent governments within our territorial limits."*

The Five Tribes and others seeing the writing on the wall "absolutely decided to take a united front and oppose the allotment

THREE RACES, TWO CHOICES, ONE HISTORY

of their land and the termination of tribal governments," wrote Dr. Brad Agnew, a history professor at Northeastern State University in Tahlequah. Though the tribes tried several venues of resistance and delaying of the inevitable, eventually the tide of the struggle turned as the federal Dawes Rolls of the Five Tribes closed on March 5, 1907, superseding all previous Indian citizenship rolls. Oklahoma became a state on November 16, 1907, and for decades there after the tribal peoples of Oklahoma would struggle to survive. Over all, allotment of tribal lands stripped Oklahoma Indian nations of about twenty-seven million acres.

When the state of Oklahoma was created in 1907, the tribal governments were dissolved in large part, and the Indians found themselves living on lands which although had been promised to them as their exclusive home now constituted only 5% of the population of the new state; Indians were adrift in a sea of settlers, graft, and dissolution of tribal cultures. The tribes tried their best to rebuild again following Oklahoma statehood in 1907. Though federal paternalism suppressed their constitutionally guaranteed tribal sovereignty, they managed as they could to grasp what self-determination they could. Of an estimated ten thousand American Indians who served in World War I, many of them hailed from Oklahoma. Oklahoma Indians became U.S. citizens upon receiving land allotments, but sadly many would ultimately lose their lands by fraudulent dealings from white opportunists.

The cutting characterization of the allotment process results as described by Angie Debo was the atrophied rubble of Indian sovereignty which the nations fought their way up from starting with the Indian Reorganization Act (IRA) of June 18, 1934. Also known as the Wheeler-Howard Act, this federal legislation addressed the status of Native Americans and was something of the "Indian New Deal". It was assistance sorely needed as in 1921 Oklahoma's Adair county would earn the distinctions of having the highest concentration of full-blood Cherokee Indian residents, as well as being the poorest county in the United States, and the decade of the 1920's would see deepening poverty among the tribal people of Oklahoma adrift without tribal governmental recourse for their challenges.

The gist of the Indian Reorganization Act (IRA) legislation was to reverse the long standing goal of assimilation of Indians into American society. The Act restored to Indian tribal governments the management of their tribal resources such as land and mineral rights and provided for some economic development for Indian reservations.

Alaska and Oklahoma were added under another separate law in 1936, as Native American tribes in Oklahoma had their communal "Indian jurisdictional lands" subjected to allotment and their titles extinguished, so Indians there did not have any reservations left. The legislation, called the Oklahoma Indian Welfare Act of 1936, known as well as the Thomas-Rogers Act, extended the 1934 Wheeler-Howard or Indian Reorganization Act to include those tribes within the boundaries of the state of Oklahoma, to facilitate restoration of Indian tribal communities, return land to the nations, facilitate tribes to rebuild their governments, and encourage Native American cultural renewal.

Seeking to "strengthen, encourage and perpetuate the tribes" and their historic traditions and culture the act changed the course of decades of federal Indian policy. As part of the new approach, Indian communities again began to see efforts at allowing the exercise of self-determination. The tribal governments remained under the tight control of the Bureau of Indian Affairs of the Department of the Interior, with native people having little input in relation to the affairs impacting them.

For decades the remnant functions of Indian government in Oklahoma would rock along in an extremely limited way, with programs such as relocation in the 1950's and the termination policy following that like many that would come and go, the cycle of alleged change and stifling paternalism continuing through the mid twentieth century. In 1975 hopes for changes returned when the Indian Self-Determination and Education Assistance Act supported a strengthening of tribal governments, who began to again exercise powers of self-government, including business councils, and many established tribal courts with law enforcement powers exercised. These tribal governments made some progress in the last decades of the twentieth century.

THREE RACES, TWO CHOICES, ONE HISTORY

Cultural revitalization took root among many of Oklahoma's Indian communities, with the Pan-Indian cultural movements of the early and mid-twentieth century expanding into a dynamic social scene, as well as cultural activities generated by the Indian Arts and Crafts Act of 1935 and the 1978 American Indian Religious Freedom Act, spurred many communities to bring out again traditional sacred ceremonies so crucial to expressing Native community identity.

Many tribes now host an annual heritage day, festival, or homecoming, with powwows and dances again regular community activities in the late twentieth and early twenty-first century. As well the continuation of native languages is important to the survival of culture, many Oklahoma tribes have instituted preservation policies and activities, such as language classes and revitalization projects. These visible external expressions of the native American identity can mask a growing internal crises though. Oklahoma's three dozen tribes today are doing well for the most part. There remains in the social heart of many of the Oklahoma tribes, and groups with roots in the southeast, many unresolved issues related to their origins, histories, and present realities. It is most easily observed in the politics of these tribes as they become more successful economically, reemerging after generations of marginalization and federal paternalism, once again attempting to stand tall after a century of a slow crawl back to self-determination.

CHEROKEE

Once Marilyn Vann and I talked about the long and twisting road of the Vann surname across American history and into our own genealogies. The family has many who found a place in the history books among the Cherokee; there are several Joseph Vann's, my own forbearer Edward "Ned" Vann, and James Vann, the last an individual illustrative of the axis of the Cherokee identity and the racial intersections of black, white, and Indian. He lived from the 1760's through the winter of 1809 and in his time was one of the largest slave owners in the Cherokee Nation before removal, and was a man referred to in archival materials as one of "vengeful" and "excessively cruel" traits. Today his one-time home and now a tourist attraction in Georgia sports in front of the restored structure a bronze plaque which thoughtfully mentions briefly the hundreds of African slaves who once labored in the unending fields of this land that was two centuries earlier the Cherokee Nation.

A mixed blood, he would inherit his plantation from his white Scots father. He was like many of the mixed blood elites neither wholly one or the other; He "dressed like a white gentleman" but "berated whites" when they crossed him, despite being a man of color in a time when few whites would tolerate such treatment. The records reveal he was rich, arrogant, and a pro-assimilation. This was during the era when Americans authorities encouraged black slave ownership among the Cherokee, and other southeastern nations as a path towards "civilizing" the Indians. Vann's plantation and its enslaved people, along with his affluent mixed blood status and wealth would make him powerful as well as influential with whites and Indians alike. This is shown in when he died at the age of 43, he was not only one of the wealthiest men in the Cherokee Nation, but in the eastern United States at the time.

By the late 1820's the Cherokee Nation had in place slave codes akin to the ones long established among the Americans. These forbid black slaves and their children from intermarrying with Cherokee Indians, from drinking alcohol, or even owning property. Vann would die young, but 20 years subsequent to James Vann's death, the Cherokee Nation was forcibly removed by the

The Freedmen's Quandary

American government and driven west on the Trail of Tears to the Indian Territory. James Vann's son and his family were ejected from the successful plantation that James had received from his white father; they along with their hundreds of enslaved people would join nearly 2,000 other enslave people who are estimated to have marched with the Cherokee to the west.

In the Indian community the shadow of history stretches long over current lives. The past is never far away among Seminole, Creek and Cherokee people. Don Shadburn, a noted Cherokee historian shed some light about James Vann's domestic life, a narrative I found interesting as a descendant of the Catawba/Cheraw Indian "Scott" family, noted its presence among almost all southeastern tribes with ties to the Carolinas.

> "His wives included three sisters, daughters of Walter Scott, a South Carolina Indian trader-- Elizabeth Scott (mother of Delilah Vann McNair), Polly Scott, and Peggy Scott. Jennie Foster and Nancy Ann Brown (half-sister of the Scott girls) were also wives. Nancy was Joe Vann's mother."

Such a heavy hand and the institution of slavery was bound to fins those opposed to it. The Vann family would also see their holdings, human and material play a role in a slave revolt in the Cherokee Nation a decade after the arrival of the Cherokee there. The Indian Territory was alarmed when a group of twenty-five enslaved individuals from the Joseph Vann plantation, made efforts to escape to Mexico where slavery had been abolished. On November 15, 1842 the Vann plantation would find many of its formerly bound resident's fugitives from the law as they gathered with people from other plantations near Webbers Falls in the Cherokee Nation and set forth.

The escapees raided a local store and seized horses and mules, as well as several rifles, ammunition, and supplies for the journey to Mexico. Cherokee officials soon got word of their escape and a search party was dispatched to bring them back. Along the way the fugitives were joined by ten more absconding from plantations in the Creek Nation, who also sent men to join the Cherokees in pursuit of the fugitives. Confronting the party of escapees near the Canadian River, a shootout resulted with two fugitives killed and twelve captured. The twenty-one who escaped then together continued in the direction of Mexico while the Cherokee and Creek posse who pursued them returned to their communities for reinforcements.

Near the Canadian River, the fugitives met two men who were slave hunters who had in their possession eight slaves, one man, two women, and five children. These people had earlier escaped from the Choctaw Nation and were headed westward when they were recaptured. The fugitive party killed the two and added the Choctaw fugitives to their group, continuing on their way to Mexico. In fear that a general escape by other black slaves in the Indian Territory would be triggered by the escapes, the Cherokee National Council on November 17, 1842, authorized the Cherokee Lighthorse Militia to find and return the escapees.

Eighty-seven well-armed men departed to recapture the twenty-nine fugitives, whom they soon caught up with near the Red River. The posse would soon recapture the now thirty-one fugitives and soon brought all of them back to the Cherokee Nation. five of the fugitives were remanded to be held at Fort Gibson pending trial for the killing of the two slave catchers, which they were ultimately were executed for after the trial.

The Cherokee National Council ordered the remaining fugitives to be returned to enslavement by their Cherokee, Creek, and Choctaw owners. The Cherokee slave revolt of 1842 was the largest slave rebellion in the Indian Territory and the efforts by those enslaved souls to break their bonds started on the Vann plantation. This wouldn't be the last episode in the Cherokee history when the Vann name was associated with breaking loose form the will of others. Marilyn Vann and the court case that bears her name will likely be remembered well.

The playing out of the politics of Cherokee Nation, like all Indian politics, had mesmerized me for years, and the last few decades reveal a tribe on the move and returning to health, but not without growing pains. In the late summer of 1997 I heard there was to be a "direct action" concerning struggles within the Cherokee Nation capital over poor governance, that there would likely be trouble in Tahlequah. I had heard through coworkers at my job at Whirlpool Tulsa that some other Indian activists would be there and especially one, Chad Smith a tribal prosecutor for the tribe, was known for his tenacity concerning native issues.

Disputes within the leadership of the nation was coming to a head. Removed from office by what some said was a corrupt administration, the Cherokee Marshals and the Court Justices targeted by the administration continued to show up at the old Cherokee courthouse in downtown Tahlequah despite their having been let go, trying to find a way to overcome the persecution heading their way.

In the wake of the 1996 election, Cherokee authorities were questioned as to the possibility that federal funds were used inappropriately by the then Principal Chief Byrd administration. Sensing smoke they may have started looking for the fire; while this initial investigating was underway they began to look into whether Byrd had improperly paid hundreds of millions in legal fees to a firm that his wife's brother-in-law worked for. Slow to turn over the requested documents to the Cherokee National Council, Byrd's reticence led to a court-ordered search of his office.

This search by the Cherokee marshal service must have been too close to home for Byrd, because he fired in short order the 15 Cherokee Marshals who were involved in the seizure and copying of the records. To make matters more difficult he also made clear in statements that he would not acknowledge the high court of the Cherokee Nation's authority. Byrd was charged with obstruction of justice, but before that could stick his supporters on the National Council -- with a one-vote majority -- impeached the Judicial Appeals Tribunal, the tribe's highest court. This was all the lead up to a fisticuffs at the historic Tahlequah courthouse.

As I arrived with a Euchee friend, a co-worker and fellow traditional Stompdancer who was also interested in the unfolding situation, we saw a fracas starting up as we pulled up, soon with sirens and angry looks on all sides. We never could make it to

CHEROKEE

where the tiff was playing out as policemen were everywhere, and the incident resulted in the arrest of Chad Smith, who was there protesting too. Such was my introduction to Cherokee politics, and the birth of my daughter Sehoy a month later would take me away from what was to be quite an internal struggle for the government of the Cherokee Nation. My cousin Pony Hill was working at the Jack Brown Center in Tahlequah with Indian youths and we both were attending meetings in Sapulpa the Euchee Tribe were holding in regards to their fight for federal acknowledgement, separate from the Cherokee Nation. Going to stomp dances at the Wakokiye Tallassee Ceremonial Grounds, I heard second hand from a couple of Cherokee friends, of the fallout of the troubles of the administration of Byrd and the stirrings of another fight on the horizon was being talked about.

While Pony was working for Cherokee Nation at the Jack Brown Center at Sequoyah School working as a youth counselor for the tribe, we would note changes unfolding that made us both believe Cherokee Nation was going through something of a rising consciousness and a feeling of confidence in the tribe's future. The Jack Brown Center was established in 1988, and was a center for Indian kids from any federally recognized tribe living in the Midwest area. The politics were just getting raw in Cherokee Nation when Pony decided to go back to Florida.

Through Pony I met Chooch Christie who I would see at Stompdances at Wakokiye or at Redbird or Stokes. Chooch Christie would tell me that if there was ever a day in the Cherokee Nation that lacked political intrigues, he had never heard of it. He waded into politics himself but things turned out badly. In the early part of 2001 we would lose Charlie "Chooch" Christie by his own hand, us both having once been active American Indian Movement guys had led to us becoming friends. He was 43 years old and the help the he gave Indian kids at Jack Brown Treatment Center will always be appreciated and remain with those who knew him. Pony and I both accompanied him that Tuesday afternoon after the funeral to the Freewater Cemetery.

Ronnie Bluebird, another full blood Cherokee friend, had some insightful views of things happening in Cherokee Nation in the late

90's. Ronnie and I used to work together and I often gained insights from his views of his nation, relatives, and friends, that was hilarious. He never tired of providing an everyday workingman sounding board on the affairs that were swirling across Cherokee Nation in those years. My interest then was piqued by a conversation we had one afternoon about the Freedmen Cherokee and his view that they were not Cherokee. We would spend many a long shift at the Tulsa Whirlpool plant discussing the merits of Oklahoma, citizenship, and the tribe.

Sometimes another elder we worked with, Mrs. Mouse would throw into our conversation her own as she passed. It didn't escape my notice then that none of these lifelong residents of the Cherokee Nation whom I knew and worked with thought the Cherokee Freedmen were a part of the same tribe, or were in anyway connected to them. This led to my beginning to pay attention to the infrequent mentions of Freedmen in the Tulsa World and other papers, and to speak to people I would meet at work or on the campus of Rogers State University where I began a B.S. degree program in sociology in 1998. From my studies I knew the dynamic of Cherokee national sovereignty versus the rights if individual Freedmen. I wanted to know more.

I first crossed paths with a lady named Marilyn Vann during my genealogical work into my own Vann family origins. Being a descendent of Edward "Ned" Vann, Sr. (1720 - 1770), I was working on figuring out the ties between the mixed blood Cherokee and Creek Nation families I descend from and came across her story of struggle to secure her citizenship in Cherokee Nation. She grew up in Ponca City, the daughter of a janitor and Baptist preacher, in talking with her she always knew she was native but didn't get to grow up close to her family's heritage among the Cherokee. She was a capable contender for those adversaries at the Cherokee Nation who would come to rue her name; being a former government employee for the Treasury Department, she came to the struggle with some legal training background and familiarity that readied her for the onerous amounts of research on the Freedman issue she would put it.

CHEROKEE

She started at the local university law library and in archival databases from the Daily Oklahoman and Tulsa World newspapers. She began to build a resistance to stop the slow slide of the Freedman further from their heritage as Cherokee and against forces within the community seeking to push them out entirely. She told me she was taken aback to get a rejection letter from the tribe when she tried to enroll more than a twenty years ago. Her dad was an original enrollee on the Dawes Roll which to her meant she was eligible for citizenship into the tribe.

She went to court and after a legal battle was able to in 2005 finally secured that enrolled status. She wasn't satisfied with how things were though and wanting to get secure citizenship for her fellow Freedmen, she went back to court and started an advocacy organization, the Descendants of Freedmen of the Five Civilized Tribes Association. In 2007, Cherokee Nation voters approved a constitutional change that made it harder for the Cherokee Freedmen to gain standing in the tribe. She rose to the challenges of the politics of the situation. The struggles that were ahead would be many and years and untold effort would be spent by her and other activist to finally establish securely the place of the Freedmen in the Cherokee Nation.

The words of the US District Judge in his ruling in Cherokee Nation v. Nash as to whether the treaty gave the Cherokee Freedmen "all the rights of native Cherokees", and Freedmen people like Marilyn Vann a secure place in the nation came as a confirmation of a social struggle by her and others that was long, hard, and uncertain.

> *"The Cherokee Nation can continue to define itself as it sees fit but must do so equally and evenhandedly with respect to native Cherokees and the descendants of Cherokee freedmen. By interposition of Article 9 of the 1866 Treaty, neither has rights either superior or, importantly, inferior to the other. Their fates under the Cherokee Nation Constitution rise and fall equally and in tandem. In accordance with Article 9 of the 1866 Treaty, the Cherokee Freedmen have a present*

> *right to citizenship in the Cherokee Nation that is coextensive with the rights of native Cherokees."*

With such long reaching historic ties to the past and the importance of the legacy of generations gone by found in Native American identity, its striking the vehemence which the subject of those descended from people enslaved by the Cherokee and in some cases likely the Cherokee who owned them, can illicit. For a people for whom history is an aspect of identity and genealogy is a pastime, the reaction of Cherokee I spoke to about the role of slavery in their tribe was muted. Few wanted to speak about the presence of the slavery in Cherokee history, most plead ignorance of that long ago institution, yet all were quick to contribute their view of the Freedmen's efforts to remain citizens of the Cherokee Nation. Tribal politics has long been a subject of favorite discussion in Indian Country and some would say is a blood sport among the Cherokee.

In what has been described as one of the more hotly contested political matches in the history of the modern Cherokee Nation, the Freedmen of that tribe continue to be Cherokee, despite strenuous efforts by some in Cherokee leadership to strip them of that status. For Cherokee Nations Freedmen descendants, the long-running dispute affecting hundreds of families of descendants of former enslaved people held within the Cherokee Nation finally came to a close in 2017 as the Cherokee Nation of Oklahoma accepted a landmark federal court ruling confirming their citizenship rights as the Cherokee Freedmen, according to Cherokee Nation's Attorney General Todd Hembree[13]. The acceptance was a long time in coming though. The Freedmen enrollment applications are again being executed after a 10-year delay in their processing due to the dispute. Hembree, the tribe's top legal official, said in a statement the Cherokee Nation unequivocally accepted the court's ruling.

> *"The Cherokee Nation respects the rule of law, and yesterday we began accepting and processing*

---

[13] https://www.indianz.com/News/2017/08/30/freedmen-win-landmark-ruling-confirming.asp. **Accessed 3/26/2018**

CHEROKEE

citizenship applications from Freedmen descendants, I do not intend to file an appeal."

For the nearly 3,000 Cherokee Freedmen citizens who had at one point been expelled and then returned to the tribal rolls then just as suddenly found themselves again disenrolled, the roller coaster rides of the last several decades have finally slowed down. The struggle had several twists and turns as in 2006 about 2,800 Cherokee Freedmen descendants secured citizenship in the Cherokee Nation after a historic tribal court ruling allowed for it, but new applications were set aside after the tribe in 2007 changed its constitution, amending it to explicitly deny Cherokee Freedmen their right to enroll going forward, similar to the actions taken by the Creek and Seminole Nations to keep Freedmen off the tribal rolls. A ruling from Judge Thomas F. Hogan settled the issue once and for all for the Cherokee when his decision stated that a treaty signed in 1866 subsequent to the end of the Civil War guaranteed Cherokee Nation citizenship to the descendants of former enslaved people in the Cherokee Nation.

In the early fall of 2017, the U.S. District Court decided for the Freedmen descendants and the U.S. Department of the Interior in the Cherokee Nation v. Raymond Nash et al. and Marilyn Vann et al. cases. The ruling clarified that according to Article 9 of the Cherokee Treaty of 1866, the Cherokee Freedmen descendants indeed have present rights to citizenship in the Cherokee Nation, which are coextensive with the rights of those Cherokee "by blood"[14].

Important issues that have emerged from the Freedmen's struggles include the issue of "blood" lineage among tribes such as the Five Tribes of Oklahoma, and the role of government officials and accuracy of records utilized in regards to determining tribal membership today. Previous to the Dawes Commission, the Cherokee as a community often included people from previous rolls and people of non-Cherokee ancestry as members of the

---

[14] Cherokee Nation v. Raymond Nash, et al. and Marilyn Vann, et al. and Ryan Zinke, Secretary of the Interior ruling, August 30, 2017

Nation. Such persons and communities, from former captives to members by adoption were considered fully Cherokee in past generations. Many are surprised that as many as 50 white people historically were adopted into the Cherokee Nation and were categorized as "Cherokee by Blood" in the tribe's base roll used to determine citizenship, the Dawes Roll. The Cherokee have long long been a multi-ethnic people.

The Cherokee absorbed many tribes during the historic era, including the Natchez who have been part of the Cherokee Nation for hundreds of years. The Delaware and Shawnee were two tribes of several who in days gone by found refuge among the Cherokee, and whose descendants are citizens of the Cherokee Nation by way of the Delaware Agreement of 1867 and the Shawnee Agreement of 1869. Recent efforts to gain separate federal recognition by such groups have met with mixed reactions within the Cherokee Nation, yet such ethnic as well as racial diversity in the Cherokee community has long been a hallmark of their tribal identity for many generations. Taylor Keen, a Cherokee Nation tribal council member, said that historically, citizenship in the Cherokee Nation has been an inclusive process and that the Dawes Roll was anomalous to that.

> *"it was only at the time of the Dawes Commission there was ever a racial definition of what Cherokee meant. The fact that it was brought back up today certainly tells me that there is a statute of racism"*[15].

The Freedmen's struggle brought many pressing and critical issues to the fore. An issue important as any is that of the dangers involved in any tribe breaking a treaty protected by Article Six of the United States Constitution. Daniel F. Littlefield Jr., the director of the Sequoyah Research Center at the University of Arkansas at Little Rock, forwarding that the Treaty of 1866 established unequivocally for Cherokee freedmen their rights as

---

[15] Daffron, Brian (2007) "Freedmen descendants struggle to maintain their Cherokee identity", Indian Country Today, March 30, 2007. Accessed 3/26/2018

CHEROKEE

citizens of the Cherokee Nation, and the case "should not be made into a racial issue"; indeed, it should be understood as resting fully on the sovereignty of tribal governance as a pre-existing government to the American federal government, with a government to government relationship defined through the Constitutional provisions that establish the fiduciary trust relationship between federally recognized tribal and the American federal government.

Some assert that because the Cherokee Nation does not determine tribal membership on the basis of blood quantum[16], arguably to some a more obviously racialized marker of group inclusion, as many tribes across the country do, but instead on lineal descent which is a genealogical based measure of belonging, the crossroads of race and sovereignty encountered in the struggle are all the more significant here.

But the waves made by the political struggles and posturing in the case reached out to touch many tribal governments concerns. In 2007 members of United Keetoowah Band of Cherokee[17] heard their Principal Chief George Wickliffe share his concerns, like that of many other tribal leaders, about threats to sovereignty because of the Freedmen case, stating that the Cherokee Nation of

---

[16] Certificate Degrees of Indian Blood (CDIB) are issued by the Bureau of Indian Affairs to certify and quantify the applicant's American Indian ancestry, in many instances using documentation from state-certified vital records. The CDIB "white card" provide a degree of ancestry by tribe, such as "1/4 Choctaw and 1/8 Cherokee." Important to note is that CDIBs are not evidence of tribal citizenship; individuals can have a CDIB and still not meet the standards for enrollment set by tribal governments. The opposite holds true as well: individuals like the Cherokee Freedmen may qualify for tribal citizenship, even if they do not possess a CDIB. A "white card" will show tribal enrollment with a tribe.

[17] The United Keetoowah Band of Cherokee Indians in Oklahoma (or UKB) are a federally recognized tribe of Cherokee Indians headquartered in Tahlequah, Oklahoma. The UKB members are mostly descendants of "Old Settlers" or "Western Cherokee," the Cherokee who migrated to present-day Arkansas and Oklahoma about 1800 before the forced relocation of the Cherokee Nation from the Southeast in the late 1830s under the Indian Removal Act.

The Freedmen's Quandary

Oklahoma and its adamant efforts at refusal to abide by the Treaty of 1866 endangered the government-to-government relationships of other Indian tribes, which had struggled to make the United States federal government live up to its treaty promises.

The UKB and the CNO have a long running feud which the Freedman controversy didn't help. Some of my friends who are enrolled UKB members and are full blood, traditional people from the ceremonial ground near Kenwood, Oklahoma found it laughable that a tribe "as white as the Cherokee Nation would cast judgement on Freemen folks". It is true that countless tens of thousands of enrolled Cherokee Nation of Oklahoma citizens have Indian blood quantum fractions in the hundreds or thousands of percent, and that the vast majority of its well over quarter million enrolled members are near total white ancestry. One person is reported to have a CDIB of 1/2000's.

There are some who see the case of the Santa Clara Pueblo v. Martinez as the Supreme Court's view in ending the only federal court avenue for Native Americans who find their citizenship in their tribal nations revoked, namely the Indian Civil Rights Act. The individual Native American is now at the unrestricted power and is vulnerable to whatever whims of political leadership is put in control of tribal government. The power to disenroll persons based on racial status holds the potential to do great harm if it is ever established. The Cherokee Nation, with the Freedmen controversy, demonstrated that very potential in its treatment of tribal citizens who trace descent from enslaved people of the Cherokee Nation.

Most relevant of the repercussions of the Freedmen controversy though may be the social and emotional cost to the ties between the Freedmen and the Cherokee Nation.; many have voiced in interviews that they feel that they have been "gradually pushed out of the Cherokee Nation", that the process has left each generation less aware of its rights and its history, and that they are not wanted. Freedman activist Reverend Roger H. Nero stated these feelings of alienation in 1984.

CHEROKEE

> "Over the years they [Cherokee Nation officials] have been eliminating us [Freedmen] gradually. When the older ones die out, and the young ones come on, they won't know their rights. If we can't get this suit, they will not be able to get anything" (Sturm, 2002).

Another Freedman descendant critiqued the degree of disconnect he perceived by the Cherokee Nation of its own legacy. Freedmen descendant and journalist Kenneth Cooper said as much in his narrative "Slaves to Denial", published on the Afrocentric blog TheRoot.com, in 2009.

> *"By rejecting a people whose history is so bound up with their own, the Cherokees are engaging in a massive case of denial. The history of every family descended from Freedmen reflects close relations with Cherokees, down to some last names still in use today."*

As a descendant of the influential Vann family of the Cherokee Nation myself, I have had good conversations with my friend Marilyn Vann, president of the Descendants of Freedmen of the Five Civilized Tribes, about the place of Freedman people in Indian society. She and her organization have fought ceaselessly for the heritage of the Freedmen community, and was one of the primary plaintiffs in the lawsuits to defend it and clarify the community's status. With the decision by the courts she told NPR the costs of doing the right thing are not easy, but are necessary.

> *"There can be racial justice...but it doesn't always come easy, what this means for me, is the Freedmen people will be able to continue our citizenship ... and also that we're able to preserve our history. All we ever wanted was the rights promised us, to continue to be enforced."*

Bearing a flag for justice like the many civil rights giants on whose shoulders she stands, Marilyn has been tenacious in her nonstop efforts to secure a fair hearing for the Freedmen's case. Tribal sovereignty, which she acknowledges as important and foundational to Native American identity has been used as primary argument against the inclusion of people like her at times. in 2006 and 2007, when opposition to Freedmen inclusion as part of the tribe took place on a wider scale than ever before, a time marked by public speeches, grassroots petitions, e-mail campaigns, and letters to the editor in the tribal newspaper, seeking to exclude families like her own, she and others redoubled their efforts for justice. As anthropologist Circe Sturm contends the realities are complex and at times dissonant.

> *"in positioning civil rights as something separate from, or even against, tribal sovereignty, we obscure the fact that in the lived experience of people like the Cherokee Freedmen, both claims exist side by side and actually depend on one another.[18]"*

the uniqueness of the indigenous position towards the Indians place in American politics and society is well known. The rallying cry of "American Indian tribes are nations, not minorities" (Wilkins, 2001) is heard clearly as it is for federal Indian law, where "American Indian" has been repeatedly upheld as an explicitly political rather than racial category[19]. Through the recent decades of struggle among the Freedman and black Indians of the Five Tribes, a movement of the importance of organizing, acknowledging and advocating for their rights as the unique communities they are has grown.

Their identity as citizens of their nations has been challenged, assaulted, and in some revoked, yet the same battle is creating culture warriors like Vann and Graham who are energizing the unique identity of the Freedmen with a contemporary relevance and a call to duty for the preservation of heritage like never before. With Vann's Cherokee and Graham's Creeks, the holding of persons of African ancestry in bondage was an affair not unlike that of the neighboring white men, but the story of the Seminole

---

[18] https://indiancountrymedianetwork.com/news/native-news/still-waiting-cherokee-freedman-say-theyre-not-going-anywhere/
[19] (see Rolnick 2011 on Morton v. Mancari 417 U.S. 535 [1974]; and Strong 2005 on The Indian Child Welfare Act, 25 U.S.C. § 1901–1963 [1978]).

and the relationship with the African peoples who found a place among them is not as simple an affair in some ways.

To many of the Freedmen descendants I spoke to over the past decade and a half, the ongoing pursuit of justice they endure is about acceptance of their status as fellow Cherokee by others, a recognition of the shared tribal identity as Cherokee. For many involved on all sides of the Freedmen controversy in the enforcement of a century-old treaty looms the modern day benefits included with being a tribal citizen, such as free health care, educational scholarships, and housing assistance. Exclamation that black "non-Indians" were unjustly suing tribes just for economic benefits was the source of some of the racially charged statements and perceptions of the less informed among the concerned parties.

Some more traditional oriented Cherokee who shared their view of the Freedmen controversy with me coached the mindset of some in positions of Cherokee leadership during those difficult years as being "internally colonized". Some assert that once settlers claim the land as their own, they are here to stay, and the ideas of race they brought have become integrated into the Indian community through the colonization process, even to the point of internal acceptance of views that are inherently non-native. "Colonialism is not some event that happened in the long ago past, a moment of invasion now long finished" said a relative active in the Cultural Survival organization, a nonprofit group based in Cambridge, Massachusetts, which is dedicated to defending the human rights of indigenous peoples.

To risk sounding academic, "it constitutes an ongoing relationship in which settler's descendants actively maintain forms of social domination, enabling them to continue to occupy native lands", whether in North and South America, Africa, or Australia, in perpetuity he said. "The oppressive relationship that is constructed is justified by way of racialization of persons". Racializing identity for an Indian tribe is antithetical to the bedrock of the constitutionally founded relationships tribes count on to survive, as political entities predating the United States. If the sovereignty of the Cherokee Nation is defined principally in political terms as a government with a unique status constructed of specific rights connected to particular lands, historical experiences, and legal matrices, then the physical presentation ought to be irrelevant; should it matter if Cherokee citizens appear, sound, and act like popularized conceptions of them entertained by the non-Indian public?

the case of the Cherokee Freedmen during the recent struggles like generations before reveals how conceptions of racial identity across varying interactions influenced the Cherokee Nation in its exercising of its sovereign powers. Most visible was the relations between the Cherokee Nation and outsiders to the community, which was apparent as soon as citizens of the Cherokee nation voted to disenfranchise the majority of the Freedmen from eligibility for enrollment. With that, many outsiders commented on them as being "racists" and asserting that Cherokee who held a racially based idea of Cherokee identity were "acting white".

Most dangerous to the Indian community was the view that tribes acting so were no longer authentic in their Indian identity to deserve the federal funds that as a federally recognized tribe the Cherokee Nation is mandated to share in. The Congressional Black Caucus wading into the fray, confronting directly the Cherokee Nation's sovereignty and the vocalized promise to cut its funding and federal recognition, are publicly visible fault lines for Indian Country that all tribes take serious. The erosion of integrity between the Cherokee Nation's elected leadership and its own citizens was another of the impacts that came to light; the vote in 2006 concerning the Freedmen's status represented a push to connect Cherokee citizenship to a racially based distinct status, linking it to an explicitly Indian rather than a Cherokee national identity.

More than most other tribes, the extremely white admixed citizenship as a majority of the membership of the Cherokee Nation should refrain from such racial approaches to identity. "As much mixing as most of these around here have been doing for the longest, you'd think us Cherokee would be more accepting...I guess not," said my friend Jesse Hair, a full blood from Braggs Oklahoma as we talked about the issue between rounds one night at a stomp dance. "It's no easy story how we wound up like we are today". It is a complex story indeed. Manipulations of the terminology and arrestment of the issues in terms many deemed inaccurate and some as misleading by Cherokee leadership failed the high standard of leadership the people of the tribe deserved, said one CNO employee caught up in the machinations during an interview. Among the Cherokee Nation citizenry as a whole the issue of the Freedmen's status revealed a type of "historical amnesia" as one researcher put it. In interviews and the press, many Cherokee voiced significant ignorance about the long history and shifting cultural and tenuous legal status of the Freedmen in the Cherokee Nation.

This collective ignorance of their own role in the debate about an issue as crucial as citizenship revealed how the average Cherokee citizen is in a more vulnerable position than most realize. *"The truth is that the practice of slavery will forever cast a shadow on the great Cherokee Nation."* Wilma Mankiller was foretelling the future as well as describing the past century when she said those words. Few could imagine that is happening to "black" Cherokee citizens today could happen to the hundreds of thousands of "white" Cherokee who are the majority of the enrolled membership of the Cherokee nation. Not many of these "white" Cherokee were able to accept the Freedmen as fellow Cherokee people, as "relatives" and long-time components to the diversity that is the Cherokee Nation, said one person interviewed.

During the struggle, the subtle but unceasing rhetoric against the inclusion of the Freedmen by not only representatives of the tribal government but as well even more racist propagandizing from individual Cherokee persons, led to the Freedmen being stripped of a historic tribal inclusion, recognition and sovereignty they deserved in a multi-ethnic nation as that of the Cherokee of Oklahoma. When on August 30, 2017, U.S. District Judge Thomas Hogan reinforced an important historic treaty clause that has for more than a hundred years defined the Freedmen of the Cherokee Nation as citizens of the tribe, the acknowledgment of their status also confirmed the bedrock of the Native American identity as one political, not racial. When he ruled that "the Cherokee Freedmen's right to citizenship in the Cherokee Nation is directly proportional to Native Cherokees' right to citizenship," one more link in a long chain of decisions that created the framework of the federal-tribal relationship was forged.

The assaults on the "national" identity of the Cherokee using the race card is no new affair. In 1883, only 17 years after the Civil War era treaty that established the Freedmen as citizens of the Cherokee Nation was ratified, there were those in the Cherokee Nation who initiated a steady attempt to abate the "rights of native Cherokees" to those of the Freedmen. This was a circumstance that came to the fore frequently when Cherokee Nation lands were up for sale or remuneration by authorities. The monies garnered from such events, all too common in the lead up to Oklahoma statehood, was only intended for "Cherokees by Blood" asserted certain leaders and tribal citizens with a racialized view of who was, and was not Cherokee.

The records reveal that there was then like now jurists, those in the legislature and Indian agents who frequently challenged this view and asserted an alternate view even under threat of punishment. Is it really surprising than looking back on the last few decades of the playing out of the Cherokee Freedmen controversy that "blood politics" again made its appearance, the ghosts of challenges past carrying over into the contemporary fight over the identity of the Cherokee Freedmen. Chief Bill John Baker's emergence as the victor in a heated and divisive political struggle with a message that all Cherokees no matter their bloodline come from "one fire", was but a manifestation of the inclusive that lies at the heart of the Cherokee identity as a people.

From the early 1830's and the Cherokee Nation v. Georgia, when the Cherokee Nation hoped for relief by a federal injunction against legislation passed by the state of Georgia depriving the Cherokee of rights within Georgia's asserted boundaries, the Supreme Court has upheld that special constitutionally grounded relationship. When the Supreme Court did not hear the case on its merits but instead ruled that it had no original jurisdiction in the matter, as the Cherokee were a dependent nation with a relationship to the United States like that of a "ward to its guardian," as said by Justice Marshall, the echo from that long ago case joins the most recent of Cherokee Nation v. Nash, et al, in a

CHEROKEE

legal whole. Once again the Cherokee Nation is at the legal "cutting edge" in the struggle over identity. As my friend Marilyn Vann said after the dust settled from the "groundbreaking" decision by the court, "this is a new day, and I am hoping that the tribe can come together in unity where we are no longer Cherokee Freedmen, but simply seen as Cherokee."

CREEK

In 1866 A treaty negotiated between the Creek Nation and the U.S. federal government in the days after the Civil War conveyed to those enslaved in the nation their freedom. They were no longer held by individual Creek tribal members in bondage and the federal government told the governments of the Five Tribes to extend to these newly freed people full tribal citizenship. For the various groups of Freedmen of the Five Tribes they would meet differing fates as free people. The Muscogee (Creek) Nation Freedmen lost their citizenship in 1979, as did the Choctaw Freedmen in 1983. The Chickasaw Freedmen were never granted full citizenship in the years after the Civil War and the Emancipation. The 21st century would find many of those descended from the Freedmen of the Creek Nation feeling that they have been cheated out of part of their heritage, and some began to seek redress for the mistreatment that they experienced when turned away from their attempts at tribal enrollment.

Some of those descended from people enslaved generations ago are today looking at their options in light of the several other tribal versus Freedmen episodes; the Freedmen of the Muscogee (Creek) Nation of Oklahoma have a strategy other than seeking to have their Muscogee (Creek) Nation citizenship rights restored as did those among the Cherokee or Seminole. Instead, some have formed the "Muscogee Creek Indian Freedmen Band" and have sought federal recognition from the federal Bureau of Indian Affairs of their group.

Seeking to preserve and protect the unique history, heritage and genealogy of the Muscogee Creek Indian Freedmen who were removed to Indian Territory (later Oklahoma) on the Trail of Tears, to promote interest and participation by sharing genealogical information with members, researchers, and the general public, the organization has been meeting to facilitate its mission. Seeking also to provide assistance "as an educational resource to researchers through lectures, workshops, conferences, and museum exhibits, and to educate the public regarding the African Creeks' political rights as citizens of the Creek Nation, as defined by the Creek Treaty of 1866 (Article 2)", the group is a resource for the many Creek Freedmen seeking to know more. the group has been active in their mission to restore political autonomy to their community, and the historical record shows their people have in past, long been active in tribal affairs among the Muscogee Creeks for many generations.

> *"The history of the Creek Nation is littered with the presence of the Freedmen and their descendants. In the aftermath the Civil War, when the Creek Nation had not yet surrendered and was in chaos, a former slave (of Yamasee descent) by the name of Cow Tom emerged on the scene by establishing order in the camps at Fort Gibson. He was an Interpreter for Creek leader, Yargee[20]"*

Leguest Choteau Perryman is among one of the most celebrated Creeks of African ancestry that the Freedmen group points to as an example of their contributions, as an extra Census Bulletin from the Department of the Interior Census Office, Washington D.C., United States Printing Office, 1894 shows.

> *"The Five Civilized Tribes in Indian Territory, The Cherokee, Chickasaw, Choctaw, Creek, and Seminole Nations – Paragraph 6 reads, "The negroes are among the earnest workers in the Five Tribes. The Creek Nation affords the best example of negro progress. The principal chief, virtually a negro, comes from a famous family in Creek annals. His name is Leguest Choteau Perryman"[21].*

As the following excerpt from Congressional Records dialogue stated before a committee held on November 21, 1878 at "Muskogee, Indian Territory" where the committee met with Senators who were present, the chairman and Mr. Grover, the President. The black Indian speakers shared on behalf of the Creeks Leaders Porter, Hodge and Stidham.

---

[20] Daniel F. Littlefield, Jr.; Africans and Creeks
[21] http://www.1866creekfreedmen.com/media

CREEK

"*Jess Franklin, having been duly sworn, was examined. By the Chairman:*

QUESTION: What is your name?

ANSWER: Jesse Franklin.

Q. Are you a Creek? A. Yes, sir.

Q. Were you a slave? A, Yes, sir.

Q. Were you born here? A. I was born among the Indians.

Q. Where? A. In the state of Alabama.

Q. What office do you hold in the nation. A. I am a judge of the Supreme Court.

Q. Judge of the Supreme Court, are you? A. Yes, sir.

Q. How many colored men are on the bench besides you? Any? A. No sir, I am the only one.

Q. What are the other four? A. Creek Indians.

Q. How long have you been a judge? A. Three years this fall.

Q. What is your salary? A. Five dollars per day.

Q. While in session? A. Yes, sir.

Q. How often do you sit? A. As long as there is business to attend to.

Simon Brown, having been duly sworn was examined.

Q. Are you an Indian? A. Yes, sir.

Q. Were you born in the Creek Nation? A. Yes, sir.

Q. Were you a slave? A. Yes, sir.

The Freedmen's Quandary

Q. What office do you hold in the Territory? A. I am a Senator

Q. Do colored people get their full share of the school fund? A. Yes, sir, so far as allowed by treaty...

Q. How many members of the Senate are colored men? A. Three that belong to the Senate.

Q. How many belong to the other House? A. I cannot tell exactly all there are. But there are three that belong to the house I belong to besides myself[22]*.*

WPA interview with Simon McIntosh, "Sugar George and Jesse Franklin (Creek Freedmen) were my uncles and both members of the Creek Council. They, "Coon Creek" Harry and twenty-one other delegates were sent on a mission to Washington. There, the colored delegates were pushed forward to speak for the Indians. They seemed to be able to better express the wishes of the Creek Tribe than the Creeks themselves. The Government officials called upon said: We want to talk to the Indians. What are these colored men doing the talking for"? The Creek delegates said, "What's the matter? We want them to talk for us"

Examples of those once enslaved yet recovering and moving forward with their hopes, are many. The first Creek Freedmen to enroll with the Dawes Commission was one Paro Bruner, who at the time was at-least 75 years old. He was given the number 1 for his Dawes roll number, and was a formerly held in slavery by Wash Barnett, a Muscogee Creek Indian. In the Creek Nation in 1866 following the Civil War and the emancipation of all those enslaved there, Paro Bruner became a respected Creek Nation political leader and even was an elected Creek National Councilmen in the House of Warriors for many years representing the Canadian Colored Tribal Town. His wife Aggie Laudrum was listed as number 2 on the Dawes Roll. One Freedmen said that the

---

[22] Indian Pioneer History, Jerome Emmons, Interviewer, Page 403-404, August 10, 1937.

ties between the Freedmen and the Creek people are deep, and the legal relationship between African and Indians are long complex.

> *"After the Civil War African slaves in the United States were made citizens of America by virtue of the 13th, 14th and 15th amendments. Slaves in the Five Tribes were made citizens of their perspective Nations as well as their descendants by virtue of the 1866 Treaty. Citizenship is not about race or blood. It is a legal binding contract. It's that simple."*

The Creek Freedmen controversy that unfolded in the Muscogee (Creek) Nation in Oklahoma, much like that of the "Black Seminole" and the Cherokee Freedmen, is one example of the struggles for identity and the impact of the "one drop rule" concerning any persons' ancestry still present even today in the eyes of some critics[23]. Between the years from 1981 to 2001, the Creek Nation had membership regulations that permitted individual applicants to present documentary sources from differing sources to establish proof of their claims for citizenship, but such documentation must exist to be provided; many mixed Indian-Black freedman were simply listed as Freedmen with no documentation of their Indian ancestry recorded. In his ***Contested Territory Whites, Native Americans and African Americans in Oklahoma, 1865-1907*** Murray R. Wickett addresses the extensive intermarriage among the African and Indian Creeks.

> *"It was only among the Seminoles, and to a lesser extent among the Creeks, that intermarriage was fairly commonplace. One contemporary commentator noted that among the Seminole and Creek tribes, "intermarriage became so common, so than now (I have it on the best authority) there is not a Seminole family that is entirely free from negro blood; and there*

---

[23] The one-drop rule is a social and legal principle of racial classification that was historically prominent in the United States asserting that any person with even one ancestor of sub-Saharan-African ancestry ("one drop" of black blood) is considered black (Negro in historical terms).

> *are but three Creek families, some make it two, that are of pure blood[24]."*

Since 1979, membership in the Muscogee (Creek) Nation is based on documented lineal descent from persons listed as Creek 'Indians by Blood' on the Dawes Rolls, compiled more than a century ago. The Muscogee (Creek) Nation does not have a minimum blood quantum requirement, and as of 2018 has nearly 80,000 members, less than 2000 of whom are "full blood" Indian (though multiple tribal ancestries). There are no "pure blood" Creeks today, as reading the century old narrative above would lead one to expect after many generations of intermarriage with others, including African Creek citizens.

The criteria for MCN citizenship is that applicants must be traced back to a direct ancestor listed on the 1906 Dawes Roll as Creek "by blood", by issuance of birth and/or death certificates[25]. With the recording of the Dawes Roll several types of enrollment categories by the authorities were instituted, including Creek by blood as well as Freedman. There is little evidence that much effort was made to verify the self-identification of those enrolling, other than the enumerators personal judgement of the applicant's racial

---

[24] Contested Territory Whites, Native Americans and African Americans in Oklahoma, 1865-1907 by Murray R. Wickett

[25] The criteria for Muscogee (Creek) Nation Citizenship is that applicants must be "Creek by Blood" and trace back to a direct ancestor listed on the 1906 Dawes Roll by issuance of birth and/or death certificates. Another words If an applicant's parent is enrolled as of 1981, then the Citizenship Office will review the documents that were submitted for the applicant's mother or father's enrollment as well as the entire lineage to the original enrollee. If no one is enrolled between the applicant and the original enrollee, then the MCN requires the death certificate of the original enrollee and birth certificates and/or death certificates with supporting documents of each person thereafter leading up to the applicant. Initial documents that need to be submitted for the applicant include the completed Citizenship application, the State Certified Full Image Birth Certificate, copy of social security card and if 18 years or older, a State Identification or Driver's License. If any Birth or Death certificate has been delayed, amended or is computer generated, a supporting document is required; such as a social security abstract listing parents, school record also listing parents or any legal documents listing parents and signed by a judge.

CREEK

makeup in many cases. In his book Wickett goes on to say on page 16 that Freedman strongly identified with their Creek heritage.

> *" on the one hand, some freedmen were part Indian themselves. They tended to be proud of their Indian heritage. One settler remembered that freedmen did not consider themselves black but rather emphasized their tribal affiliation."*

In 1979 the Muscogee Nation Constitutional Convention voted to restrict qualification for citizenship in the Muscogee (Creek) Nation to those who could prove descent from "Indian by blood". Applicants had to be able to show direct descent from a forbearer documented on the Dawes Commission roll in the category of "Creek by Blood". The Dawes Commission roll was initiated in 1893 as a registry that the American federal government established to identify citizens of the Creek Nation at that time to allot out the tribe's communal lands and create a dissolution of the reservation system and tribal government.

"The General Allotment Act is a mighty pulverizing engine to break up the tribal mass" said Teddy Roosevelt, and this it did effectively, crippling Indian self-determination for decades and crippling efforts at preservation of tribal languages, identity, and community. In 1979 a vote on citizenship requirements for the Muscogee Creek Nation excluded descendants of those recorded only as "Creek Freedmen" on the Dawes Rolls. The decision by the MCN to exclude Freedman has been challenged in court by those descendants, according to the 1866 treaty, of "Creek Freedmen."

The Freedmen as a community are one of several identifiable groups within the Creek Nation jurisdictional area then and now and were, like Creeks "Indian by blood", listed on the Dawes Rolls. Some Freedman descendants can prove by archival documentation in other registers that they had forbears with Creek blood, but those who came to be Freedmen were listed on a separate register, regardless of their proportion of Creek ancestry. Grant Perryman, a Creek Freedmen from California relates the true depth of the ties that bind todays Freedmen people to their Muscogee Creek past.

> "My gr x 3 grandmother, Melinda Cow Tom married John Jefferson who served time in the Mvskoke Creek Government in the House of Warriors. John Jefferson was placed on the Dawes "Freedmen" Roll. His parents were listed as Jeff Randle and Betsey Randall. His full brother, Manuel Jefferson, was placed on the Dawes "Blood" Roll as 1/4 Mvskoke and his parents were listed as Jeff George and Betsey George. Their full brother, Silas Jefferson, was placed on the Dawes "Blood" Roll and was listed as 1/2 Mvskoke and his parents were Jeff McNac and Betsey McNac. Silas Jefferson was also known as Hotulko Mikko, roll #3694, cc#1141, and was a member of the House of Kings & 2nd Chief. John Jefferson and his wife Melinda are also listed on the 1860 Census on page 7 #78 and John is listed on the 1870 Loyal Creek Abstract on page 2 #130. Note that although he is not listed as Creek, he is listed as a free "colored"[26]."

With outsiders doing the judging often based on the physical presentation of the applicant, research efforts have shown there were many of known Indian blood who were registered simply as "Freedman" among the Creek as well as Seminole, Cherokee, and other Five Tribes. The classification of these individuals as simply Freedmen did not acknowledge the unions and intermarriages that had taken place for generations between the several ethnic groups that made up the Creek Nation. Controversially, before the change in the registration codes, Creek Freedmen could use existing registers and the preponderance of evidence for qualification for Muscogee (Creek) Nation citizenship, and were to be facilitated by the Citizenship Committee in attempting to adequately document and gain tribal enrollment.

The Creek Freedmen did as the Cherokee Freedman and black Seminole, and have legally challenged in many courts their

---

[26] http://www.thecreekfreedmen.com/id7.html

exclusion from Muscogee (Creek) Nation citizenship in actions still pending in some cases. In the general American society even one drop of (perceived) African ancestry has led to many being regarded as black regardless of social identity, and with the compilation of the Dawes roll similar situations unfolded among the Five Tribes of Oklahoma as well, wherein those with visible African ancestry were often recorded simply as Freedmen with little attempt to establish known Indian ancestry or genealogical ties.

In, 'Creeks and Seminoles,' written by J. Leitch Wright Jr. there is section dedicated to "black Muscogulges", and in that chapter, he forwards how the racial admixtures among the Muscogee (Creek) were too complex to easily measure with mixtures of red, white and black ancestry made it impossible to assign accurate blood percentages to the principle Muscogee (Creek) racial components. Though it sounds like the Southeastern U.S. during the Pre-Removal era was a melting pot of races and culture, by the first part of the 19th century, a few wealthy Creeks owned slaves and white attitudes towards race had been adopted.

At a Freedman Association meeting at a library in an African-American part of Tulsa, I heard stories from many Freedman of the legal and social challenges they face. Listening at a gathering in the Creek Nation capital in Okmulgee I hear passionate narratives of experiences shared as a half dozen elderly African Americans recount the exclusion they and family members have endured. At one meeting, Ron Graham is speaking of the import of addressing the Indian community directly, of Creek Freedman and Black Indians working together to overcome the racial barriers he feels repeatedly thrown up against his community by more assimilated portions of tribal government. Graham tells me of his dad, an elder others remembered as well. "Blue" Graham lived like a traditional Creek does, dancing at the stomp grounds near the town of Arbeka, speaking Creek and participating in the life of the Indian community as a member of it, regardless of complexion. Graham tells me his old people handed down to him an appreciation of the identity as Creek people to include himself as one.

His conviction is clear in his voice when he speaks. Like others who take the time to parse the complexities of the allotment process, he understands the bigotry and confusion at the time the Dawes Rolls were taken led to his current predicament, the rush to statehood all but trampling the rights of Indians and people of color, the crowds seeking to profit off the demise of the Indian governments leading to unscrupulous behavior by friends and strangers alike in some cases as the dispossession of the people of the Creek Nation and the Indian Territory played out. The President of the Muscogee (Creek) Indian Freedmen Band, Ron tells me his group sent their first letter requesting federal recognition as an independent tribal nation in 2012, submitting over 8,000 documents to Washington.

He said his MCIFB is an organization seeking to represent descendants of Freedmen Creek who lost citizenship status shortly after the MCN government was reorganized in 1979, *"when they changed the Constitution but that was the start actually because it was in 1981 when they established the citizenship roll,"* Ron said in an interview. Article III, Section 2 of the MCN Constitution in part states, 'Persons eligible for citizenship in the Muscogee (Creek) Nation shall consist of Muscogee (Creek) Indians by blood whose names appear on the final rolls as provided by the Act of April 26, 1906 (34 Stat. 137), and persons who are lineal descendants of those…'

> *"…we don't want to get into the same thing the Cherokee Nation, this day are going through."*

He said the others of the Five Tribes have their own Freedmen issues and similar treaties from 1866 and while the Seminole Nation has retained their Freedmen citizens, others like his own Muscogee (Creek) Nation and the Cherokee Nation have passed tribal laws that removed them. In an interview with Sterling Cosper of MvskokeMedia.com, Graham clarified why his association is going the directions they are, and seeking the path of greater independence as a group rather than of inclusion in a nation that may Freedmen feel does not want them.

CREEK

> *"We decided to do this, go this route trying to get our tribe because we don't want the problems that exist with other tribes and we don't want the problem once we get in, are they going to kick us out again…I'm just talking for the people who are members of our (MCIFB) association," he said. "Now I can't speak for all Creek Freedmen descendants."*

He pointed out just how the Freedmen were active in the society of the Muscogee (Creek) Nation over time and have contributed significantly to the rebuilding of the it after the Civil War's decimation. Many Freedmen served the interests of the people of the Creek Nation with distinction.

> *"They were judges. They were attorneys. They were tribal legislators. They were in the House of Kings, House of Warriors, they were doctors, teachers. They were Lighthorse Police and of course, they were loyal citizens."*

From excerpts *from "Condition of Certain Indian Tribes. Testimony of G. W. Stidham, Eufaula, Ind. T., May 25, 1885 before the US Senators",* we can see the place of the Freedmen in Creek society clearer, and hear in the words of those that new them their contributions.

> *…"the treaty provides that such and such a class of colored people shall be citizens with equal rights with us in the country---those that we held as slaves."*
>
> ….
>
> *Q. Have you some officers who are negroes? --A. Yes, sir. Some members of the council are negroes, and we have one negro supreme judge, and the captain of the light horse is a negro.*
>
> *Q. Have you any negroes who are school teachers? -- A. Yes, sir.*
>
> *Q. Is there any discrimination as to holding office, or any other privilege in the nation? --A. No, sir.*

The Freedmen's Quandary

Q. A few moments ago you spoke of a supreme judge being a negro --A. Yes, sir. (Justice Jesse Franklin, Creek Freedmen, Dunn Roll #1268)

Q. What is the proportion of representation in the council between the negroes and Indians? --A. The representation is governed by towns in which they originally lived, instead, as it should be counties. They are represented by the old towns. They are represented in that way, and the colored people form three towns, according to the population. In one town there is about 1,400 and the representation, of course, is very large.

Q. How many colored members are there in the council? --A. I suppose we have about twenty in one house.

Q. From one town? --A. No, sir; from three towns.

Q. Then representation in the house is based upon population? --A. Yes, sir.

Q. I will ask you, in the house of warriors what is the proportion of strength between the negroes and Indians? --A. I think they have nearly twenty representatives out of ninety.

Q. How is it in the upper house? --A. They have three members in the upper house.

Q. Of how many members does the upper house consist? --A. It consists of forty-five members in all.

Q. Was the negro judge of the supreme court elected by the Indians? --A. Yes, sir.

Q. He could not have been elected without the consent of the Indians? --A. No, sir.

....

CREEK

> *Q. If I understand you, you consider the negroes who came in under the treaty of 1866--that is to say, those born and raised among you, whose homes are here and who came in as Creeks under the treaty--are citizens? --A. Yes, sir; that is what the treaty says...*
>
> *Q. Your council consists of two houses? --A. Yes, sir.*
>
> *Q. The upper house is called the house of kings? --A. Yes, sir.*
>
> *Q. And the lower house the house of warriors? --A. Yes, Sir.*

After the war the Freedmen like other citizens of the Creek Nation began to rebuild their lives and communities. Creek Freedmen led the effort to establish several all-black towns in Oklahoma after statehood, on top of those towns of the Creek Nation that had long been so. During the late nineteenth as well as into early twentieth centuries, black people in Oklahoma, many who were Freedmen people, would established more than thirty all-black communities in the old Indian nations territories, where they adapted to the "local environment, utilizing native horticultural and construction techniques" as one scholar stated[27]. With the benefit of new land grants from the land runs of the statehood era, these small black communities grew into major centers with "banks, post offices, trading depots, churches, schools, railways" and businesses of all sorts.

One time enslaved people were drawn to these growing all black towns as a chance to get a fresh start in life for themselves in owning property, many for the first time, and which for new arrivals made possible attaining economic independence as well as putting racial oppression where they came from behind them they hoped. With the so-called "unassigned lands" in the former Indian Territory that was now Oklahoma for settlement, and with the

---

[27] http://aliciaodewale.com/2016/02/16/creek-freedmen-and-the-formation-of-all-black-towns-in-oklahoma/

Indian lands redistributed in the 1870s through the year of Oklahoma statehood in 1907, the black population in Indian Territory quadrupled, from 19,000 to more than 80,000 as the Oklahoma Freedmen were joined by other African-American immigrants and family members.

Some researchers believe these figures do not represent the actual number of African-American immigrants settling in the Creek Nation, as they were the Seminole Nation, in the years subsequent to the end of slavery; during the four decades after emancipation, the white population quadrupled from 109,400 to 538,500. During the same time, the Native American population held at the same 61,000. This massive increase I the numbers of incoming American blacks and whites created significant consternation among all citizens red and black of the Creek Nation, who found it increasingly difficult to compete for land resources in their own territories. Within decades the citizenship of many of the Five Tribes would find themselves strangers in their own land.

The all black towns saw growth and prosperity through until the 1920s and 1930s. Impacts of the Great Depression spelled trouble for many of the black towns of eastern Oklahoma, and of the original thirty-three black towns once thriving in Oklahoma, the mid-20th century would see fewer than nineteen still hanging on. Despite their declining fortunes, there are several such rural mostly black towns still in existence today. These are communities like Boley, Brooksville, Clearview, Grayson, Langston, Lima, Redbird Rentiesville, Summit, Taft, Tatums, Tullahassee, and Vernon. Many Freedman descendants still call these towns home. Damario Solomon Simmons, a Creek Freedman descendent spoke in a recent interview of the loss of human potential to the MCN, when persons like himself could not enroll.

> *"It to me, prevents the Nation from fulfilling its full potential when you cut off a significant portion of your people that can be building a Nation up, providing their talents, their resources, their connections and their love to a Nation."*

CREEK

Some contemporary people involved in the community feel the word "Freedmen" shackles the Muscogee Creek people to stay in a certain mindset, unbecoming of a modern multi-ethnic tribal people like the Muscogee (Creek) Nation, which once had treaties with European powers as an ally and which was once larger than most European countries today.

> *"It freezes people in time, they really believe that anybody on the Freedmen Rolls is a slave and they have no Creek blood. I totally reject that."*

As the current laws of the Muscogee (Creek) Nation now stand, Simmons, even though he can document his Creek ancestry on other documents, Indian heritage he is very proud of, he is ineligible for citizenship in the tribe because his ancestor appears on the Dawes Freedmen Roll. Grant Perrymen's personal perspective of events during his generation are revealing of the deep sense of confusion and marginalization that many Freedmen and black Indians feel towards the current view of their identity held by many tribal members, entangled in red tape, racially biased paperwork, and an increasing racialization of tribal societies long home to many constituent populations.

> *"In 1979 the Mvskoke Creek Nation changed their constitution and only allowed descendants of those found on the Dawes Blood Rolls to enroll as citizens. My ancestors were at one time full-fledged Mvskoke Creek Citizens and were listed on several rolls predating the Dawes Roll. They were interpreters, government officials, preachers, teachers, ranchers, farmers, judges and ordinary men and women. They spoke Mvskoke Opvnakvn. They dressed as Mvskoke. They ate Mvskoke food and followed Mvskoke traditions. They were Vmestvlke. Brother has kicked out brother. Racism has replaced tradition. Injustice has wiped out justice. Immorality has won over morality."*

The words of another Freedmen descendent, Mary Ann (Wells) Cunningham, echoes the same grappling with the difficulties of modern tribal politics, and the seemingly illogical application of unjust measures by authorities who were once fellow tribesmen.

> *"Knowing the history of the Creeks, their hardships, misuse, abuse and all the other horrors they endured, to think that the Nation now have become exact copies of the people who inflicted their pain, tore their families apart, and taken their promised land."*

SEMINOLE

While the Cherokee and Creek Freedmen have seen complex issues arise in the struggle over their citizenship, those most exemplary of the complex matrix of race, identity, and tribal belonging at play is the "black Seminole" of the Seminole Nation of Oklahoma, a group of Freedmen who unlike those among Cherokee have not been so fortunate in keeping their people as "fully a part of the tribe" that they have been a part of for two hundred years or more in some cases. With different histories of tribal inclusion behind them as populations within the tribes of Indian Territory and Oklahoma, the Freedmen of the Cherokee and those of the Seminole seem to have divergent paths ahead as well.

As of the high court's decision that the Cherokee Freedmen are and will be citizens of that nation, the Seminole Nation has as well settled its struggle over the Freedmen's place on the tribe, though not to everyone's satisfaction. We are members of this tribe and they still deny us because we are black, said one Seminole Nation Freedmen representative in a 2016 interview. Some Indian members of the Seminole Nation said that they felt that "full benefits of tribal membership should only go to those who can prove their bloodline". Such sentiments leave some black Seminole with a bad taste in their mouth.

LeEtta Osborne Sampson, a Seminole Freedmen, told me at a meeting once about her father's tribal identity card, even as the card she herself held says she has voting privileges only, and not many of the benefits of "Indian" citizens of the Seminole Nation. Like many other Seminole Freedmen, she feels the sting of the tribe's rejection that occurred several years ago, and is working to educate the Seminole people about the realities of the social dynamics that created the Dawes Roll and the Seminole Nation as it is today, including Freedmen.

The work of enrolling the citizens of the Indian Territory's "Five Tribes" and other of the 80 plus groups of removed peoples banished there was assigned to white clerks sent from Washington to set up sprawling tent villages in area towns, spreading word through local and tribal officials that those interested in claiming their tribal land allotments had to register. Once the news spread, the hastily constructed signing tables of wooden planks on sawhorses were swamped with applicants in many cases. Surprising for the Washington clerks were the thousands of what they perceived as black people who showed up. The 1890 census counted 18,636 people "of Negro descent in the Five Tribes" present in the Indian Territory. Lacking ability to speak any Native American language, the overworked clerks often relied on just eyeballing the applicants, with those who fit the stereotyped idea of what an Indian should look like, traits like ruddy skin, straight hair, high cheekbones being placed on the "by blood roll", while those with any visible African ancestry placed on the Freedmen's roll.

The roll noted each person's "blood quantum," the fraction of their parentage that was ostensibly Indian. That blood quanta number was sometimes based on offered documentation, but many times, considering the lack of accurate records and the language barrier, it was nothing more than guesswork. It's obvious then how the seeds for the conflict in the twentieth first century was laid at the beginning of the twentieth century, and the sense of injustice felt by those whose ancestors were caught in such an arbitrary and scattershot affair, with such repercussions for generations to come.

Tribal governments such as the Seminole Nation receive federal funds for programs like housing and health care based on their enrolled tribal population, and the tribe does count the Freedmen among the enrolled membership when they report those numbers to the federal authorities. A lady passionate about her Freedman heritage, LeEtta Osborne Sampson said to me on the sidelines of a regular Freedmen organizational meeting that if the Freedmen counted in tribal funding, they should share the benefits of such.

> "The principle is our heritage. This is a part of our heritage. This is not a handout. This is not someone asking for charity. This is a people that belong here.

Across "Indian Country" increasingly present federal lawsuits challenge basic notions about race, tribal membership, and historic notions of indigenous identity in America. Although many of the same issues have been addressed in the past, multiple cases over the last few decades give new urgency to the question of who is an Indian, and with controversies like mass disenrollment, changes to criteria for federal acknowledgment, and slashed funding to tribal governments on the agenda, the future is more uncertain than ever. The Freedmen controversies among the Five Tribes are but one example of the changing social landscape of "Indian Country".

The descendants of escaped enslaved African persons have been community members of the Seminole Nation of Oklahoma for generations, as they were in Florida before the tribe's removal west in the 1830's. Just a glance at the East Oklahoma tribe's governing council reveals the descendants of these enslaved peoples alongside the descendants of the native people who took them in and fought alongside them so long ago; Some Seminole have the blood of both as well as that of their common European adversaries running them. The Seminole have long been a multiracial people. What of those "black Seminole" who cannot prove the Indian blood due to the vagaries of the Dawes Roll the tribe uses for its base roll?

After generations of inclusion by the tribe there are Freedmen who no longer feel like members of the Seminole Nation of Oklahoma; on July 1, 2000, the Seminole Nation held a referendum for a constitutional amendment establishing new membership rules requiring that members had to have one-eighth blood quantum, of documented descent from an Indian member on the Dawes Rolls. The General Council prohibited representatives from the two Freedmen Bands from participating in the action. With the change, about 1200 Freedmen were excluded from tribal membership and the benefits afforded to the tribe. The Seminole Nation would find its decision didn't go far with federal authorities in Washington D.C.

The Freedmen have long been citizens of the tribe but they were denied the benefits afforded other members and in recent years have been denied the right to vote in tribal affairs. A pushback effort started in 1994 when, Freedmen in Wewoka, Oklahoma signed up for benefits, knowing they would be denied. Subsequent to a series of lawsuits, which were eventually settled when the

The Freedmen's Quandary

Bureau of Indian Affairs issued a memorandum in September of 2003 that said it would open the benefits to all members of the Seminole Nation. Representatives of the BIA explained the benefits available and said, the regulations that defined an Indian had been amended, and the Freedmen's benefits would include such things as health, schooling, clothing and burial the benefits available to all American Indians. The descendants of the Native Freedmen have in 2018 regained citizenship in the Seminole and Cherokee Nations, and though it is still limited in the former, how did the fight to regain this right occur?

Challenges to long-established beliefs about the relationship between Seminole Indians and people of African ancestry long associated with the tribe in the American West have emerged as modernity has overtaken a long historical alliance of 200 or more years. Alternatives have arisen concerning widely accepted perspectives of the Seminole and other groups' histories, some arguing that the descendants of the Seminole Freedmen of Indian Territory and later Oklahoma are a unique cultural group neither wholly Seminoles nor "black Indians", a common term applied to many. They are without doubt just one of several groups of "black Seminole" heritage.

Black Seminole descendants continue to live in Florida today, some as enrolled members of the Seminole Tribe of Florida…as long as they meet the one-quarter Seminole Indian ancestry enrollment criteria for blood quantum. Today there are about 50 Black Seminole who have at least one-quarter Seminole ancestry and live on the Fort Pierce Reservation, a 50-acre parcel taken in trust in 1995 by the Department of Interior for the Seminole Tribe of Florida as its sixth reservation[28]. There are hundreds more who live in the area but do not meet the requirement for enrollment yet consider themselves as of Seminole descent, despite lacking tribal membership.

---

[28] Mike Clary (November 26, 2007). "On Fort Pierce Reservation, black Seminoles complain of isolation". South Florida Sun-Sentinel. Accessed 3/26/2018

SEMINOLE

Additionally, there are descendants of Black Seminole who reside on Andros Island in the Bahamas, a community originating from a few hundred refugees who had left in the early nineteenth century from Cape Florida to go to the British-held Caribbean islands for sanctuary from American enslavement. Andros Island in the Bahamas would be a refuge for Black Seminoles who escaped from Florida seeking freedom, with black Seminole first landing secretly on the island in 1821. They were in search of better horizons after the Brits on Nassau fell through on their assurance they would help the Seminole Indians and Black Seminoles in their battle against Americans coming into Florida raiding villages and attacking Seminole communities. The legendary "Wild Indians" of Andros Island as they were known for generations are descendants of the Black Seminoles who fought with Osceola, and the majority of residents in the modern settlement of Red Bays on Andros Island are descended from those original exiles from Florida.

Of the several groups of Seminole origins, sometimes called the Afro-Seminole diaspora, the black Seminole of the Seminole Nation of Oklahoma live closest to their unique heritage still; yet the exact dimensions of their social relationship with the Indians they share centuries long association with remains somewhat disputed. In his book ***The Seminole Freedmen: A History*** (University of Oklahoma Press, 2007), Kevin Mulroy asserts that runaway enslaved people from plantations in Georgia and South Carolina found refuge among and soon settled alongside the Seminole Indians in Florida, in time they migrated to the Indian Territory, Mexico and Texas along with their Seminole allies and established new communities. He asserts that these "Seminole maroons" as they were sometimes called, formed their own autonomous communities led by people of African descent and established cultural identities independent of the Seminole Indians and their tribal governments (Mulroy, 2007).

A legal battle over millions in federal funding led to Seminole with Indian blood voting to removal of those known as black Seminoles from tribal rolls in the Seminole Nation of Oklahoma. One leader involved in the case said in an interview that "this has become one of the major hot-button issues in Indian Country: Who is an Indian? And, just as important, who decides who is an Indian?"

The Freedmen's Quandary

Robert A. Williams Jr., director of the Indigenous Peoples Law and Policy Program at the University of Arizona College of Law, feels that the future requires tribes to fully clarify what it means to be a Native American. Seminole people though having several descendant groups scattered from Florida, to Texas, to Mexico, and to the Bahamas, have a unique history unlike most other tribes of the more than 567 tribes that are legally recognized by the Bureau of Indian Affairs (BIA) of the United States.

The Seminole Nation of Oklahoma, and the Seminole Tribe of Florida are among the largest and best known, but there are pockets of Seminole descendants in several areas who share historical roots. Other of the "Five Tribes" of Oklahoma who once owned many enslaved people have had similar challenges by the descendants of those who were in past held captive and whose labor and bodies were exploited, with a unified Freedman descendant organization led by Marilynn Vann leading the struggle for their rights. Marilyn Vann, the President of the Descendants of the Freedmen of the Five Civilized Tribes Association, and coordinates across several tribes and communities seeking justice for the Freedmen of Oklahoma. She said once in a conversation that 30,000 Freedman are were at one point seeking citizenship in cases against the Cherokee Nation, a significant amount of potential new enrollees. Vann's father was an original Dawes enrollee, and when she applied for citizenship to the Cherokee Nation in 2001 she was taken aback by what happened, spurring her to greater involvement in the situation, and eventual leadership.

Tribal, family, and individual loyalties increasingly are fragmented by racial and cultural identity conflicts that have arisen over several decades of legal and social struggle concerning Freedmen identity. These struggles are in a context of conflict over identity and belonging increasingly widespread across "Indian Country", including several disenrollment battles raging with a dozen tribes over and sometimes pit tribal citizens with more native "blood quantum" against those with less, or in the case of the Freedmen, none. recently several tribes have been convulsed by controversy and litigation as questions of belonging and origins, a legacy of

SEMINOLE

American history and of tribal futures come into the public eye both in Indian Country and in the mainstream media.

Many of the citizens of the Seminole Nation of Oklahoma live near the poverty level, in small communities scattered in the scrubby countryside to the east of Oklahoma City. The strangling poverty of the region and the expanding fortunes of the tribe have led to conflicts of just who is a Seminole igniting political and social conflicts unknown decades ago, yet shared in several tribal communities in the region. As one would guess the possible ending of a 200-year-long alliance between people of Indian and African ancestry and in some individuals both heritages, is a touchy area; both black Seminole and "Indians by blood" were forcibly removed from their Florida stronghold the tribe fought fiercely to keep, forced west by the federal government in the 1840's during the infamous Indian removal of the majority of the members of the Seminole, Creek, Cherokee, Choctaw, and Chickasaw Nations.

These are good times for the Five Tribes of Oklahoma. Today the Cherokee, Chickasaw, Choctaw, Creek, and Seminole are among the tribes to construct their own casinos, though some tribes have seen more success than others in their success. Isolation from major population areas contribute to the lack of economic development success for tribes such as the Seminole Nation. Recent years have seen an increase of Oklahomans previously unenrolled now coming forward to seek tribal citizenship, ostensibly to get their share of the benefits of such enrollment. One example of this increased identification with Indian ancestry is found that in 1980 there were 50,000 enrolled members of the Cherokee Nation of Oklahoma; today, there are more than 300,000.

While the enrollments of the Five Tribes have increased and include in good part people who are not identifiably Indian in appearance, the tribal governments have revised membership criteria to exclude the often darker-skinned Freedmen. This has led many to see the shadow of Jim Crow still hovering over the region, with the one drop rule at work in 21st century politics rooted in an early 20th century document, the Dawes Roll. Seminole people are often cousins, with skins of different shades and who live side by side, are confronting a changing social reality in Indian America as the established ideas of nationhood and race come into conflict with a diverse past and a difficult present reality. Black Seminoles are generally considered black people associated historically with the Seminole in both Florida and Oklahoma, (as well as having population pockets in other areas as well mentioned earlier).

They have long been significant contributors to Seminole, as well as Creek society. One well remembered elder who was pointed out as a good example of this was James Coody Johnson, who was the official interpreter for the Seminole Nation as well as an advisor to Chief Halputta Micco at the time. Born in Indian Territory in1864 as the Civil War came to a close, he was an African-Creek entrepreneur, interpreter, lawyer and politician. Being an interpreter to Federal Judge Isaac Parker, after studying law (reading law) under Judge Parker, Johnson was admitted to practice in the federal courts, singular for his time. He was a leading advocate for African-American rights and dual citizen of the Creek and Seminole nations. Very active in the Creek National Council, the Creek Leader Pleasant Porter said of him at the time, "he carries the responsibilities of two nations on his shoulders" according to records at the Oklahoma Historical Society, in the James Coody Johnson collection.

During the lead up to statehood in 1907, he was president of the Negro Protection League, and worked tirelessly as a leading advocate for African-American rights. Like many of his peers he staunchly opposed the introduction of Jim Crow laws in Oklahoma. Statehood and the requirement to register for the land allotments would mark for many African Creeks erosion of much of the freedom they had gained in earlier decades under the Indian tribal governments. The Dawes Commissions practice that African descent barred applicants from being considered full members of the Creek Nation, let to divisions among its citizens after statehood, which some say still resounds today. He continued to work for the exercise of full citizenship rights by African Americans after the new legislature passed laws imposing segregation and other restrictions. He passed away in February of 1927 (Zellar, 2007).

SEMINOLE

As a group most are the descendants of free blacks and of escaped slaves who came to be allied with Seminole groups in Spanish Florida in the 1800's, and who as families have shared the fate of the Indians they were associated with. Historically, these "Black Seminole" lived mostly in distinct communities of their own located near the villages of the Indian Seminole, with black Seminole families of these communities relinquishing a part of their crops to the clan of Seminole with whom they were connected. At times some were held as slaves of particular Seminole leaders, yet these leaders were often doing so influenced by the slavery of the white southerners. The relationship between the Seminole Indians and the black people associated with their communities is complex and no one narrative captures the diversity of their historical experience.

The enslaved people captive of these leaders had more freedom than did those enslaved by whites in the South and by other Native American tribes such as the Creek or Cherokee, and often had the right to bear arms, which some did. Again their experiences were diverse as individuals and as a group. Black Seminole descendants live for the most part in small rural communities around the Seminole Nation of Oklahoma in two Freedmen's bands, the Caesar Bruner Band and the Dosar Barkus Band. Other black Seminole centers of population, on the Ft Pierce Indian reservation of the Seminole Tribe of Florida, in small communities near Eagle Pass, Texas, and with descendants found in the Bahamas, and northern Mexico as well, have different historical experiences to some degree than those from the Seminole Nation of Oklahoma.

For generations the relationship between Indian and black Seminole in Indian Territory and subsequently Oklahoma was cooperative, as it had been in Florida when the two groups fought together. Intermarriage was frequent. One contemporary commentator noted that among the Seminole and Creek tribes, "intermarriage became so common, so than now (I have it on the best authority) there is not a Seminole family that is entirely free from negro blood...[29]" The Curtis Act of 1898 allowed the Dawes

---

[29] Contested Territory Whites, Native Americans and African Americans in Oklahoma, 1865-1907 by Murray R. Wickett

Commission to dissolve the Seminole Nations tribal government. The repercussions included the division of its territory among approximately three thousand enrolled tribe members. As with other tribes the restrictions that accompanied Indian allotment did not protect their interests in the land they received. Through sale, many times by fraudulent means put over on unsuspecting Indians, many Seminole families and individuals lost their land allotments.

By the end of the 20th century though, the times in Oklahoma were changing, and social and cultural patterns and social traditions among Seminole evolving along with them. Throughout much of the 20th century Seminole and Freedmen alike accessed the little services available to their economically depressed and rural region of Oklahoma. By 1920 only about 20 percent of the Seminole tribal lands once held by them still remained in Seminole hands; while the policy of allotment was repealed by Congressional act in 1934, much damage was done during that era to the integrity of tribal culture, government, and identity. In 1935 the Seminole Nation was able to reestablish their government, and in 1970 the Seminole tribal council was reorganized to adhere closer to its traditional structure.

In that same year, the Indian Claims Commission awarded the Seminole of both Oklahoma and Florida, collectively $12,347,500 for the land taken from them by the U.S. military during the war years. The decade would witness tribal councils across Oklahoma striving to create a number of programs including day care, alcohol treatment, education, legal aid, and others. Economic developments were begun for managing forests, wildlife, and farms. Federal funds were obtained for tribal housing, however, unemployment remained high and some tribes benefitted more than others. Slowly, the Seminole Nation climbed.

Seminole Nation society today is composed of fourteen matrilineal bands, two of these bands being called "Freedmen bands," named after the former slaves who organized them. These bands structure politics and many aspects of daily life. Each band elects a chair and vice chair, who run the monthly band meeting, as well each band elects two representatives to serve on the Seminole Nation General Council. This legislative body meets at least four times a year in the General Council House, which is located near Seminole. The government of the Seminole Nation of Oklahoma is led by an elected chief and an assistant chief[30].

With the expanding economic development of tribal communities including the Seminole though, trouble began to brew. The heat was turned up when the Seminole Nation council ran headlong into legal problems with the Bureau of Indian Affairs over the windfall of land claims monies that allowed for an expansion of services. Besides exacerbating the tribal council's problems, concerns expanded into good governance and membership issues. When the monetary award was given to the Seminole Nation yet before it could be deployed into tribal programs, a tally of enrolled citizens by the SNO tribal enrollment office counted 7,500 Seminole nation citizens. With reporting of the new services going public, applications for tribal membership quickly increased.

"When we saw applications with 1/127 blood quantum, the council decided to take action," then Seminole Chief Jerry Haney said in an interview. The Seminole Nation tribal government voted to enforce a 1/8 blood quantum for citizenship in the summer of 2000. With the 1/8 blood quantum criteria for tribal membership in the Seminole Nation, disenfranchisement of the Freedmen members of the tribe would occur. Chief Haney later said that vote to enforce a 1/8 blood quantum "was what turned the council into an "illegal" one" from the perspective of the BIA. According to the Seminole Nation Constitution, such a resolution was mandated to be reviewed by the BIA for approval. The governing tribal council was convinced that because of its tribal sovereignty the tribe could do without BIA approval.

In another turn of fate that year that grabbed national headlines, the Bureau of Indian Affairs forwarded the opinion that the exclusion of Black Seminole people was a violation of the Seminole Nation's 1866 treaty with the United States established after the close of the American Civil War. They noted that the treaty was made with a tribe that included black as well as white

---

[30] Andrew K. Frank, "Seminole (tribe)," The Encyclopedia of Oklahoma History and Culture, www.okhistory.org accessed April 06, 2018.

and brown members. The treaty had required the Seminole to emancipate their slaves, and to give the Seminole Freedmen full citizenship and voting rights. The BIA stopped federal funding for a time for services and programs to the Seminole over their poor governance and failure to comply with federal law.

In a press report in Indian Country Today from August 2000 Seminole Nation Enrollment Officer Jane McKane confirmed that although the Freedmen were still enrolled members of the Seminole Nation, but they were not provided the same social services as citizens with Seminole Indian blood enjoyed. The Freedmen did have the right to vote in tribal elections previously though, a right she said says they no longer had. The reasoning behind the tribe making changes in enrollment and enforcing a 1/8 blood quantum criteria was due to the low blood quantum in those applying for Seminole Nation membership, especially in the regards to reports of the increase in services the tribe was planning, according to McKane.

> *"The blood quantum was getting so low that the people who were enrolling weren't even interested in the tribe. They (the election committee) felt like we were really getting people with no Indian blood. That may be happening from now on I think, because of marriages to non-Indians."*

The tribe found out how serious the BIA was when the Seminole Nation tribal council was reprimanded in a Sept. 29, 2000, correspondence from then-Assistant Secretary of Indian Affairs Kevin Gover. This letter advised the Seminole Nation that its governing council was illegal, due to the manner in which in it decision making process it had bypassed the Bureau of Indian Affairs in passing the 1/8 blood quantum criteria, Chief Haney said.

The illegal actions of the tribal council of the Seminole Nation in Oklahoma in 2000 to restrict tribal enrollment eligibility to those who could prove at least 1/8 blood quantum descent from a "Seminole "by blood" on the Dawes Rolls excluded about 1,200 Freedmen who were previously included as tribal members of the

SEMINOLE

Seminole Nation. The Freedman organized a legal resistance to what was happening to their community. The case became more complicated when in 2002, the Oklahoma Seminole Freedmen's case against the government was dismissed in federal district court when it decided the Freedmen could not bring suit independent of the Seminole Nation of Oklahoma. The tribe had refused to join the suit brought by them[31]. An appeal they brought before the United States Supreme Court in the summer of 2004 affirmed that the Freedmen were ineligible to sue the federal government for inclusion in the settlement without the Seminole Nation's participation, and as a federally recognized sovereign nation, the Seminole Nation could not be ordered to join the suit.

The Seminole Nation was during 2002 left without federal monies for many programs since the BIA asked federal agencies to cancel funding. The move by officials came after the Seminole Nation decided not to allow the descendants of the Freedmen to serve on the voting council. As a result, neither the BIA nor the U.S. Interior Department recognized the Seminole Nation General Council elected that year, however, the tribe passed a resolution in October reseating Freedmen descendants on the general council and in July 2000, Seminole tribal voters approved changing to the nation's constitution that would require a person to be one-quarter Seminole to serve on the tribal council. Today, the Seminole Nation of Oklahoma continues to have two Freedman Bands, the Cesar Bruner Band and Doser Barkus Band.

Each band has its own form of tribal leadership and three General Council Representatives, though the blood quantum of these Seminole Nation citizens is 0/0 as they have no (documentable) Indian blood but are the descendants of the emancipated enslaved people held among the Seminole of Indian Territory after the Civil War. For critics of the tribal position, the debate over the status of the Freedmen is still somewhat unresolved a decade and a half later. They remain enrolled tribal members, yet do not receive many of the benefits as do Indians, according to some Freedmen's perception of the treatment they receive from the tribe. For some of

---

[31] Seminole Freedmen lawsuit dismissed" Archived May 30, 2011. Accessed 3/26/2018

the "by blood" Seminole, the long history of association between the Freedmen and the Indians still doesn't equal native bloodlines, according to an interview in 2016 with tribal members like Robert McCulley[32].

> *"The position of the tribes is that if we're going to be given words and associations with things like sovereignty, and things of that nature, well then it's absolutely that tribe's business as far as who they allow as membership, I would hesitate at all to call it a race issue. It's a matter of principle and a matter of practice as far as who we are as a people and how we govern ourselves."*

McCulley like the tribal council is not disputing the Freedman's Seminole Nation citizenship, that status is clearly stated in the 1866 treaty. The full benefits of tribal membership should only go to those who can prove their bloodline. My friend Ed Culley (no relation to Robert McCulley), a Seminole Nation tribal member from Tulsa said once when I interviewed him in 2002 that the situation with the Seminole Freedmen, like that of "white Seminoles" was one that may never find adequate resolution. "There's too much history and not enough Indian too go around" for these people he said. His comments echoed the perspective of many Indians that the Seminole Nation of the future should be more about Indians and less about the past, admittedly a past full of exploitation and marginalization of both blacks and Indian people.

"None I know have much at all to do with our language and culture…" Culley went on, echoing Seminole Nation of Oklahoma Enrollment Officer Jane McKanes words from 2 years earlier that the tribe was increasingly "people with no Indian blood. That may be happening from now on I think, because of marriages to non-Indians." Many Black Seminole express that they preferred to be called such, rather than Freedmen, and the perspective is rooted in the historic reality that the two peoples were fighting side by side in

---

[32] https://indiancountrymedianetwork.com/news/alleged-illegal-council-suspended-seminole-chief-haney/ accessed 3/28/2018

SEMINOLE

the Florida swamps for survival, a struggle that continued once they were brought to Indian Territory.

> *"They fought wars, suffered, bled and died together, people of African descent with the Seminoles. That bond was very strong. 'Seminole' doesn't mean a person who is what they call a 'blood' Indian; Seminole means people of culture," Shaw said. "There were black people, there were Indian people from different tribes, there were Spanish people, all of these people were considered to be Seminoles. But in this day in time, this younger generation just bandy that word around very, very loosely. That doesn't hurt me because I know that they just don't know their history."*

Lena Shaw, a member of one of the Freedmen bands of the Seminole Nation, is proud of her heritage and feels it is very misunderstood, even by many modern Seminole. She sees the tribe as one people of many colors, all equally Seminole. That the nuanced and unique relationship between those of Indian and those of African ancestry really has no parallel among other tribes in the United States, some scholars agree.

> *"In order to keep the American people from taking the people of African descent from them, they decided to say 'We're your slaves.' The Seminoles never treated the people of African descent as slaves; they were really equals. In fact, one of them, Abraham, a famous interpreter, went with the Seminoles to Washington, DC to interpret the treaty of 1833. As you can see the relationships were very strong and the ties were very strong. These people were smart enough to stay together. They fought wars, suffered, bled and died together, people of African descent with the Seminoles. That bond was very strong. At one time the Seminole roll was one, because they were all members of the*

> *tribe, not necessarily slaves as many like to throw around.*[33]

Black Seminole spokesperson LeEtta Osborne Sampson told me at a meeting in Okmulgee that the Seminole Freedmen were getting the short end of the stick, in the view of many, that tribal governments receive funds from the BIA for things like housing and health care, allowances based on the citizenship of the Seminole Nation as a whole; the Freedmen are listed on tribal rolls and counted when the Seminole Nation reports those numbers. She believes if the Freedmen are counted, "they should be entitled to those benefits."

> *"The principle is our heritage. This is a part of our heritage. This is not a handout. This is not someone asking for charity. This is a people that belong here. This is how I was raised and been in this nation."*

By denying the Freedman access to some tribal benefits, the Seminole Nation is technically in violation of federal law, say critics of the tribal governments position, in the words of one critic. Does the 1866 treaty bestow full citizenship rights on Freedmen, equal in all aspects to those of Indian citizens of the Seminole Nation, or not? In the view of many Freedmen, full citizenship includes affordable housing, access to health care, tribally supported employment training and the like, of which they don't have equal access. Many "by blood" Seminole assert that the only citizens who should have access to those full benefits are tribal members who can document their ancestry back to "by blood" Seminole Indians enumerated on the Dawes Roll. LeEtta Osborne Sampson says that for the SNO tribal government to "change the rules after all this time is racist". She is passionate in her assertions that Black Seminole "are members of this tribe and they still deny us because we are black. But we can date back as far as 1666 that we are Seminole."

An estimated 2000 Seminole Nation of Oklahoma Freedmen are today enrolled members reports Sharon Burgess from the Tribal

---

[33] https://indiancountrymedianetwork.com/news/jim-crow-legacy-still-disrupts-oklahoma-seminoles/ accessed 3/28/2018

SEMINOLE

Enrollment Office of the Seminole Nation of Oklahoma in a 2018 correspondence. The strained relations from the past are healing. Some see in the recent grappling between the two historically associated communities of the Seminole, both struggling for what they think is right, each facing realities of modern American life in Indian Country. One view of that ongoing dialogue sees the sovereign status of Native American tribes to define their membership a fundamental central tenet of tribal sovereignty, while from a different perspective the situation involves remunerations for generations of enslavement and the importance of a tribe to keep a promise made so many years ago in the aftermath of the Civil War. Neither the Seminole Nation tribal government nor the Freedmen are stepping back from their positions on the issue.

While the Seminole who arrived in the Indian Territory in the early 1800's had to contend with western Indian incursions, slave raids, and adjusting to a new home in far way land, some Seminole continued the fight to remain in their Florida territory. Academics assert that likely fewer than 200 Seminoles remained resisting removal to the west, deep in their wilderness stronghold in Florida after the Third Seminole War conducted from 1855–1858. These few carried on secluded lives deep in the tropical wilds rich in traditional customs and a way of life of independence, separate from outsiders. In the late 1800's, the Florida Seminole did re-establish contact with authorities though, initiating limited interactions with the federal government on occasion as needed.

In 1930 they were given 5,000 acres of reservation lands in Florida, but few of the Seminole moved to the established reservations until the 1940s, most preferring the isolated way of life deep in the everglades and swamps of the peninsula. Florida was filling with people and fast developing in the post war years. The old ways of life were becoming increasingly difficult to carry on, and social isolation becoming more difficult to maintain. A faction among the Florida Seminole initiated increased interactions with the federal and state governments, and soon reorganized their tribal government, asked for and received federal recognition in 1957 as the Seminole Tribe of Florida, with the more traditional people near the Tamiami Trail receiving federal recognition as well as the Miccosukee Tribe in 1962. Scattered among the families of both groups of Indians in Florida were families of African descended people who had affiliated with the tribe for generations.

The Seminole Tribe of Florida also has its own "black Seminole" people, individuals who physically present like other black persons, yet these black Seminole, in order to be enrolled tribal members, have to have documented ¼ Seminole Tribe of Florida Indian ancestry, unlike the Freedmen of the Seminole Nation of Oklahoma who often lack documentation of their Indian ancestry on the Dawes Roll. Unlike the Black Seminole among the Seminole Nation in Oklahoma who at times express feelings of being marginalized, those in Florida on the tribal roll are fully enfranchised tribal members of the Seminole Tribe of Florida, on equal footing with other enrolled tribal members…as long as they have the required one quarter Indian blood.

One visitor described the situation among the runaway enslaved people and their Indian protectors as one more interdependent than that among any others. As an outsider who visited several flourishing Black Seminole settlements in Florida in the 1800s, he described them as "vassals and allies" of the Seminole Indians. These families have a long history as part of the Florida Seminole as some historians estimate that during the 1820s, more than 800 blacks were living with the Seminoles in distinct settlements which were highly militarized and fairly autonomous, unlike the communities of most of the slaves in the American South.

When the regional population expanded and the Seminole came in closer contact with Americans, many of these Black Seminole families would over time integrate into surrounding African American settlements, but some remained deeply affiliated with the Seminole Indian villages of the area where their ancestors first found refuge among the Indians many generations before. While in the late 1800's some of the descendants of these Black Seminole became integrated into the surrounding African American communities located nearby in their southern Florida home, others remained connected by blood and marriage to Seminole Indian

SEMINOLE

people, a tribal group who became federally recognized in 1957. It is only fairly recently that the black Seminole put down reservation roots though.

Fifty acres of St. Lucie County, Florida were placed into the federal "trust status" with the Bureau of Indian Affairs in the mid 1990's, becoming the sixth Reservation of the Seminole Tribe of Florida, and the black Seminole had a home of their own. With the establishment of this community on trust Indian lands, it became home to two dozen Seminole families, descendants of black Seminoles and Seminole Indians who have lived in the area since before the city or county were formed.

In physical presentation the Seminole tribal members taking up homes on the Ft Pierce Reservation appear to be predominately black, but for enrollment they must have at least ¼ blood quantum to qualify for tribal membership. The majority of the Black Seminole who now live on the Fort Pierce Reservation are descended from Seminole Indians Sally Chupco and Jack Tommie, and most have both Indian and African-American blood. Today the issues of race and ancestry among the Seminoles of Florida are still contentious at times. The lines of descent and from whom one originates are still important and are controversial in some circles.

To be an enrolled member of the Seminole Tribe of Florida and so have a share in the significant tribal "per cap" disbursements from the profits of the many business enterprises the tribe is involved in, an applicant must have at least one-quarter Seminole blood. The divisive nature of the arrival of more money than the community has ever known has been troublesome. The now casino-rich tribe has had to grapple with the toll on tribal unity and identity as the tribe's fortunes have improved over the decades. Today for the Seminole of Florida, the days of hunting, subsistence living, and a precarious existence in their everglades haunts are long behind them as the 3,300 members each receive monthly dividends of about $120,000 annually, and the tribe is among one of the wealthiest in the country. The fate of the Florida tribe's "black Seminole' people will, like that of the black Indians of the Freedmen bands of the Seminole or those among the Creek and Seminole hinge to some degree on politics, changing demographics, and their tenacious hold on their identity as they see it. The black Seminole of Florida are today a small but vibrant community.

The most notable differences between the black Seminole of Florida and those of Oklahoma is that the black Seminole of Florida are enrolled tribal members through their Indian ancestry, not their "black Seminole" lineages, whereas in Oklahoma the black Seminole there in many case have little if any native ancestry documentable yet all spring from black family's long residency of the Seminole Nation and in past generation's asserting their Seminole identity in culture, language, and dress. While many of the black Seminole in Florida were in large part reabsorbed into the general African American population of the region during the late 1800's and early 1900's, those in the Seminole Nation have maintained an affiliation with the Seminole Nation and were listed on its rolls. But what does it really mean to be "Black Seminole" as they prefer to be described, finding the term Seminole Freedman somewhat historically inaccurate. What is the essence of the Black Seminole identity?

Perspectives within the "Black Seminole" community itself is not unified in answering that question. The struggles over enrollment were a moment with the threads of the historic affiliations held by their ancestors now being taxed to near breaking; some of those involved in the conflict maintained they have Seminole blood yet cannot prove their ties to registered "by blood" Seminoles to the required 1/8 threshold. Others within the community prefer on preserving their identity as descendants of Africans who have a unique "Afro-Seminole" culture, history, and identity. The existence of a unique dialect among them has been documented.

First identified in 1978 as a language by Ian Hancock, a linguist at the University of Texas, the Afro-Seminole Creole is noted to be "a dialect of Gullah spoken by the Black Seminole scattered across several communities in Oklahoma, Texas, and Northern Mexico". Small communities of descendants of the Black Seminoles continue to live in Texas, Oklahoma, and Mexico. Their unique dialect likely first evolved when Black Seminoles and Seminole Indian lived together in northern and central Florida in the eighteenth and early nineteenth centuries. The language went with them when they went west. Today speakers of Afro-Seminole live mostly in Seminole County, Oklahoma, and Brackettville, Texas, in the United States and in Nacimiento de los Negros, Coahuila, in Mexico, with about 200 speakers of the language known at the turn of the 21st century (Hammarström, Forkel, & Haspelmath, 2017).

For those black Seminole in Oklahoma, despite still holding membership in the Seminole Nation, times are still tough even today. Many black Seminole members among the Seminole Nation of Oklahoma live below the poverty level and struggle for economic sufficiency, having a hard time "making ends meet" is the common refrain heard in the dusty Oklahoma towns long their home. The Seminole Nation of Oklahoma's Indian Jurisdictional Area where they live is situated in Seminole County, Oklahoma, with the entirety of Seminole County a portion of the original Seminole Nation's reservation jurisdiction, and covers approximately 633 square miles. The area like many tribal jurisdictions in Oklahoma today is a checkerboard of tribal trust property, Indian allotment lands, and small Indian and non-Indian communities, with enrolled Native Americans compromising less than a quarter of the population of Seminole County.

The Seminole County area the black Seminole call home has around 5,315 Seminole Nation citizen's resident there, according to the Seminole Nation Tribal Enrollment Office, with a total enrollment of the Seminole Nation at approximately 17,000 members. Like many tribes among the 37 federally recognized Oklahoma tribes, the Seminole Nation struggles to supply adequate services to its members due to restricted economic opportunities, insufficient funding, and other reasons. The services that are supplied are often inadequate to the need, and the black Seminole tribal members have limited access to those.

To be included in all Seminole Nation programs "like the Indians are", as one black Seminole elder told me, might could make a better life possible, since as that elder said they made the long journey from Florida too. They endured the difficulty of life in

Indian Territory and later Oklahoma as did the Indian Seminole, and according to him, many have Indian blood that was not recorded on the Dawes Roll for the same reasons that many Freedmen of several tribes were disenfranchised...any amount of African ancestry visible meant placement of the Freedmen Roll not the by blood roll. The end of the 20th century would witness among the Seminole of Oklahoma, money and identity clash in a struggle that would cost some their place amongst the Seminole people, some say. The roots of the conflict over the place of the black Seminole in the tribe reached back far into tribal history, but came into dispute first in 1961 when the Oklahoma and Florida Seminole both independently filed claims with the Indian Claims Commission, seeking compensation for tribal lands seized by the United States government in Florida in 1823 at the time of the Treaty of Moultrie Creek. This treaty had compelled the Seminole who adhered to it to move into a reservation in central Florida and relinquishing their territory to the north.

The federal authorities accepted the claims of Seminole east and west and heard them together and in 1976 awarded a total of $16 million to both tribes. The tribal officials worked for more than 10 years to allocate the funds, which facilitated negotiations between the Oklahoma and Florida Seminole groups and leading to more interaction than the tribes had experienced in over a hundred years. Disagreements over the apportionment of the land claims funds for the Seminole were many and a slow process of attempting to allocate the money fairly led eventually in 1990 to the groups acceptance of the Seminole Nation of Oklahoma receiving three-quarters, based on early records from 1906-1914, when members had blood quantum, and the Florida Seminole to receive one-quarter, based on a reconstructed early 20th-century census. By 1990, the entire monetary settlement awarded was valued at $46 million with interest.

While the Seminole governments in Florida and Oklahoma had resolved their dispute over who received how much money, within the Seminole Nation of Oklahoma the struggle was just beginning. The Seminole Nation of Oklahoma tribal government did not want to apportion any funds from the settlement benefits to Seminole Freedmen members, since in their view the black Seminole had not been legally recognized in 1823 as members yet, a view which led to two Freedmen's Bands of the Seminole Nation filed suit against the Department of Interior in 1996[34]. As legally members of the Seminole Nation since 1866, Freedmen Seminole were supposed to be party to all benefits the Seminole Nation offered the BIA asserted. The Freedmen case was dismissed from federal district court subsequently. The court asserted that the Freedmen could not bring suit without the Seminole Nation's joining, and the Freedmen legal team fought this up the chain but in 2004, the US Supreme Court affirmed that they could not sue without participation of the Nation.

The black Seminoles posited that the Bureau of Indian Affairs acts as trustee of the $56 million land settlement fund, and the black Seminoles said it should assure that they were not the victims of discrimination by tribal officials due to their racial background. In legal documents related to the case, the black Seminoles' legal team asserted federal officials and "Seminole by blood" tribal leaders with racist intentions "plotted to exclude" the black Seminoles. The Department of the Interior legal representatives and Seminole leaders both refuted such intentions in recorded interviews stating that all decisions were made in an effort to distribute the funds as Congress mandated in the settlement requirements. These assertions fell on unbelieving ears when lawyers for the black Seminoles' uncovered a series of memorandums penned by federal authorities from the 1970's to the 1990's, documents allegedly revealing measures to deceive Congress.

With the Seminole Nation asserting its land claim in 1976, governmental bureaucrats at the Bureau of Indian Affairs generated a historical narrative of the black Seminole that concluded that in the eighteenth century some of the once enslaved African escapees "became essentially free under the Seminoles", writing in the report that the "very close relationship" between the 2 groups continued in the 1800's as they struggled to stay in Florida despite governmental efforts at removal of all Seminole from the peninsula. The Seminole Nation did have sovereign immunity

---

[34] William Glaberson, "Who Is a Seminole, and Who Gets to Decide?", New York Times, 29 January 2001, accessed 3/26/2018

The Freedmen's Quandary

from lawsuits, so the black Seminole community brought suit against the Interior Department alone in the first suit it initially filed in court in 1996 to gain access to funds set aside to compensate the Seminole for lands taken from them in the east.

the legal struggle that followed the report, concluded that the formerly enslaved people ancestral to today's Seminole Nation of Oklahoma Freedmen did not own the land in Florida at the time the American federal authorities through military actions against the Seminole Indians seized it in 1823. The black Seminoles were not a party to that transaction as they as a group were recognized as members of the tribe in a treaty with the federal government in 1866 upon their emancipation by their Seminole Indian owners. The lawyers for the Freedmen said that treaty actually recognized a long standing relationship that had already existed. Seminole "by blood" Tribal leaders asserted that the post-Civil War federal government forcibly made the conquered and decimated Seminole nation, like the other slave holding tribes in Indian Territory, accept the formerly enslaved blacks as tribal citizens, a measure which slowed the tribe's economic opportunities for years to come.

The parameters of the case were complex, with status of the black Seminoles in 1823 critical to shaping the decision in 1976b y the federal Indian Claims Commission. It concluded that 1823 was the date of the federal seizure of the Florida land, and as such Congress should make a compensation payment to the "Seminole Nation as it existed in Florida" in 1823, including all its descendants at that time. The documents related to the case include those generated by Bureau of Indian Affairs beginning in the 1970's, which reveal Seminole "by blood" leaders voiced reservation about the distribution of any payment the tribe might one day receive with the black Seminole.

Seminole Nation's chief, Jerry Haney, coached the dispute in terms of one political rather than racial in nature. His assertion was that the Seminole Nation refused the participation of the black Seminole in the funds disbursal partly because modern descendants of the historic black Seminole, unlike their ancestors who had dressed as Indians and spoke the Seminole's Muskogee language, no longer adhered to a primarily Seminole identity culturally, and that many had drifted away from identification as active participants in the Seminole community and identity. In an interview Haney said that the Interior Department officials had told the "by blood" Seminole that the funds were to compensate for the lands confiscated by the federal authorities and "the blacks were not landowners."

As the case moved its way through the courts, it invoked more and more a growing sense of uncertainty as to the overall meaning of native American identity in many communities in Oklahoma, and in other regions. By 1990 the case would find efforts to cut the black Seminole out of the $56 million settlement become explicit according to press reports from the Freedmen's lawyers. Eventually the fact that the wording appropriating the land claims monies said it was "for the benefit of the Seminole Nation of Oklahoma," which meant the black Seminoles were still unclear as to their status until it was resolved once and for all.

Reversals and sharp changes in tack would mark developments in the case as the courts suggested that only Seminoles by blood could have been members of the Seminole Nation's ancestral group in 1823. "Presuming the plaintiffs have no Seminole Indian blood, they cannot legitimately claim harm from exclusion of funds to which they are not entitled'" the lawyers said; 1998 would find the government triumphant in a trial court ruling dismissing the case on the grounds that" the Seminole tribe was an indispensable party that could not be sued because of its sovereign immunity".

Eventually a referendum was passed by the Seminole Nation governing council that stripped the black Seminoles of tribal membership, with the reaction by the Interior Department being a declaration that the Freedmen's disenfranchisement by the Seminole council was illegal. The department would not recognize any Seminole tribal government that did not include the black Seminole, and meant that the federal government could restrict or stop payment of federal funds to the Seminole tribal government if the situation was not resolved. Eventually the series of legal actions in the lawsuits ground to a near standstill, but the Bureau of Indian Affairs issued a memorandum that said it would open the benefits of the settlement to all enrolled members of the Seminole Nation.

The Freedmen's Quandary

In 2000, the Seminole Nation made moot the hopes of many when it voted to restrict citizenship to those of one-eighth blood quantum, which excluded numerous Freedmen Seminole who, although likely descending from an Indian ancestor, had only a Freedman ancestor listed on the Rolls as the white registrars often classified all persons of any visible African ancestry as Freedmen, even if the individual person in question had Seminole Indian ancestry and was at that time considered an Indian member of the Seminole Nation.

Described by Dr. Henry Louis Gates Jr. *as "a group of people whose fighting spirit and search for freedom took them to far-flung places in North America"*, the black Seminole have much to be proud of in their history. The black Seminole in Oklahoma, Texas, and Mexico have historic ties going back to 1845, when most Seminole Indians and Black Seminoles had been resettled in the Indian Territory, where they were expected by federal authorities to reintegrate with the Creeks. When the Seminole came under the control of the Creeks, the larger tribe tried to seize black Seminoles and re-enslave them, which the Seminole resisted. Although both groups were in the early years of resettlement in Indian Territory subjugated by the Creek Nation, the new life there was much worse for the Black Seminole. Some chose to leave "the nations", and move beyond return of the federal authorities, and subsequent events led to many black Seminole leaving the Indian Territory for Coahuila, Mexico, in 1849, led by John Horse.

Also known as Gopher John, he was among the principle leaders in black Seminole community affairs for over half a century. He was a wise counselor to several Seminole Indian leaders, at one time served as an agent of the U.S. government, and even became a Mexican Army officer. He served his black Seminole as a warrior, diplomat, and patriarch. He often represented the interests of his unique people in Washington, D.C. and in Mexico City as well. During his long life he would fight against the Americans, the French, and many Indian tribes. A survivor of three wars, four attempts on his life, and the never ending pursuit of slave hunters, he is still a symbol of the tenacity to survive of the black Seminole people.

While little is known of John Horse's early life it is thought that by 1826 he was living in his Seminole Indian owner's village near today's Tampa Bay, Florida. During the Second Seminole War, 1835-42, he initially led black Seminole against American military forces in Florida during the conflict. Offered the promise of gaining his freedom, John Horse agreed to surrender and remove west with the Seminole in March of 1837. In the new home for his people in the Indian Territory, John Horse at times served the army as an interpreter and on occasion as a negotiator between the military officials and the Indian tribal leaders[35]. When Horse was approached by the authorities to assist in convincing those remaining Seminole in Florida still resisting their relocation to the Indian Territory to give up their fight and accept being moved to the west, he did. He met with an old associate of his, the famed Seminole war chief, Coacoochee, and after long talks was able to eventually convince him to accept the governments terms and come in[36].

Horse returned to the Seminole Nation in 1842, having successfully completed his work for the Army. His actions must have spoken well of him, for the Seminole Nations leadership voted to grant freedom to him in the next year. This was the least they could do in consideration of his valuable services to the Seminole Nation during their long war of attrition in Florida, and afterwards in getting reestablished in the Indian Territory. Trouble soon emerged for the Seminole now in the Indian Territory because they had been relocated on lands already allocated to the Creek Nation, most likely a result of the U.S. government's failure to realize the long standing separation of the two parties. the parties who would in time become Seminole were a loose

---

[35] Journal of a Tour on the "Indian Territory": Performed by Order of the Domestic Committee of the Board of Missions of the Protestant Episcopal Church in the Spring of 1844. Domestic Committee of the Board of Missions. 1844. p. 15.

[36] James Shannon Buchanan (1951). Chronicles of Oklahoma. Oklahoma Historical Society. p. 163.

association of Creek, Apalachicola, Euchee, Alabama, Yamasee, and other remnant bands who had separated politically from the Creek Nation nearly a century earlier.

With their political break form the Creek leadership, many of the founders of the Seminole had relocated themselves into then Spanish Florida. Even while many maintained to some degree ties with their relatives to their north in the Old Creek Nation, lands that would eventually be overrun by settlers and become parts of the states of Georgia, Alabama and part of the Carolinas, they forged a new nation for themselves that would become the Seminole Nation. As we have addressed earlier, the assimilated mixed blood class among the Creek much like those among the Cherokee had adopted the American institution of chattel slavery, whereas on the whole, the Seminoles had not. The tribally oriented Seminole as a whole maintained a very different lifeway than the other of the Five Tribes. The blacks among the Seminole were more allies than property.

The sudden presence in the Indian Territory of free blacks among the Seminole threatened the enslavement system among the Creek and Cherokee mixed blood elites. Having been placed on Creek land and under the nominal sovereignty of the Creek tribal council initially, the Seminoles situation caused tensions to rise and the relationship between the two tribes to deteriorate. The free black Seminole threatened the slave-holding situation among the Creeks and brought into question the status quo they had established, transplanted from a similar situation in the Old Creek Nation to the new Indian Territory.

The black Seminole nearby was viewed by the Creeks as tempting their own slaves to challenging their captive status, and also made them targets for those looking to possess more slaves, even if by re-enslaving black Seminole. Slave raids by Creeks and other Indian groups, as well as by non-Indians soon started, seeking the easy profit of snatching black Seminole and selling them into chattel slavery. They invaded the Black Seminole villages seeking to enslave any they could seize, and taking the lead to defend his people that he would exhibit throughout his life, John Horse organized armed resistance to the raids, an armed black man fighting back definitely something the slave raiders were not used to. The preying on black Seminole would be a constant challenge to the security of the community and a point of dispute between the tribes throughout the years leading up to the Civil War and emancipation.

John Horse and his long time Indian ally, Coacoochee would in 1844 journey to Washington, D.C. with a delegation of Seminole leaders to petition for a separate territory for their tribe to be given for the Seminole alone. Forwarding that the Seminole were and had been a separate tribe for over a century, they hoped to secure the support they needed, but failed to do so. In 1845 and 1846 Horse made several trips to the American capital to present his people's plight to President Polk. He appears to have gained an audience to the president, with the support of none other than his former enemy, General Jesup, in confirming the unfair nature of the treatment of the Black Seminoles.

The General likely felt responsible since he had been the one who promised the Black Seminoles freedom upon ending their hostilities and coming in. Despite their work, no one in the federal government was willing to intervene. Horse asked that his people be allowed to return to Florida, or transported to Africa, or sent anywhere other than Creek Territory. With disappointing results the delegations repeatedly returned to Indian Territory, the Seminole still uneasily encamped on the Creek lands, still at the mercies of their one time allies.

Horse, had again displayed the leadership traits that he was known for, traveling back to the Americans capital on his own initiative and acting as a servant to an officer's brother. The point of his trip was to seek redress from General Jesup, whom he had negotiated with in Florida during the Seminole War, and to ask him to fulfill his earlier promises of assistance for Horse's people. The capture of Osceola under less than honorable conditions stood in the minds of all who had witnessed the betrayal of a parlay under a flag of truce. The General, doubtless feeling the effect of having been involved in the treacherous act that took down Chief Osceola, could not overcome politics as they stood though.

Soon though General Jesup journeyed to Indian Territory, being now Quartermaster General for the entire U.S. Army. On the grounds of Fort Gibson began work on a newly constructed project Jesup had planned, and so many black Seminole moved from their two communities, those of Deep Fork and Little River, closer to the fort to work on the construction underway. Many remained near the fort due to the continuous assaults on their communities by slavers from among the Creek and Cherokee Nations. The unjust social realities and the tenuous nature of their freedoms in Indian Territory came into stark relief soon enough for the black Seminole when John Mason a southerner, ruled in relation to a previous question of the status of the black Seminole many of whom understood there was an agreement between the tribe and the government that they had been "freed' in exchange for promises to lay down their arms in Florida and remove to the Indian territory, which they did.

The new ruling asserted that as most of the Black Seminoles were descendants of past fugitive slaves fleeing bondage in the colonies by going to Spanish Florida, and thus legally still considered born into enslavement, General Jesup's decree after the Florida conflict that black Seminole who surrendered were free had *"illegally deprived their Seminole owners of their legal property"* and that such an affair not be supported by the federal government. Many of the black Seminole had agreed to lay down arms and surrender peaceably with the thought that they would be free in the west. Their actions had without doubt weakened the Seminoles' ability to fight. This agreement that many black Seminoles had agreed to was now without warning "retroactively" revoked (Schneider, 2007).

More similar to a feudal dependency as those held by the Seminole most often lived in their own communities, there was little difference in how the Indian Seminole lived and the lives of their black Seminole "captives". the Second Seminole War would lead to significant changes in the Seminole social order, as past traditions broke down due to the fighting and the Seminole became small and mobile bands of guerilla fighters always on the move and for the most part living off the land. IJ the new realities there was

SEMINOLE

little distinction between Indian tribal members and their so-called slaves as both fought for their freedom from American dominance.

Life would change yet again in the new lands the Seminole settled on in the Indian Territory, when the Seminole were obliged to settle on fixed lots of land and take up settled agriculture, first on Creek lands and eventually on their own in the new "Seminole Nation". Then the chattel slavery adopted by those slave holders in the Creek Nation and among other displaced tribes from the south began to appeal to many of the Seminole, especially individuals who were becoming more assimilated since arrival in the territory. Some of this may have been due to the influence of the Seminole sub-agent, Marcellus Duval, who sought and advocated for legal reinstatement of alleged Seminole property rights over the black Seminole and one time allies they had fought with against a common foe.

It was soon an open season by slave raiders out of the nearby communities to assault black Seminole settlements. 280 Black Seminole people among them John Horse and his family were again in danger of enslavement. The politics of the black Seminole community was dark and their social position worsening as Horse allied with Coacoochee again as the two struggled to halt the rise of pro-Creek chiefs among the Seminole leadership and the accompanying diminishing of hopes for the black Seminole to find security. John Horse led his people to a new settlement, instead of taking his people to the site Duval the Indian agent had selected for them close by his agency. Horse and another leader called Toney Barnet, settled on the Little River at a new community he named Wewoka. He selected the site more distant from the Creek and the Seminole agency than Duval had counted on, erecting defensible barriers and fortifications to hopefully impede the parties of slave raiders who set their sights on the black settlement. Things for the black Seminole would not improve.

John Horse would marry Susan July in 1840, the daughter of a black Seminole scout and interpreter. He saw the writing on the wall for the continued freedom of his people in the Indian territory, and considering he had established an alliance with other Seminoles who wanted to be away from the Creeks and federal control, they planned to depart Indian Territory for the border in November 1849, heading for northern Mexico. They came to this drastic decision because even for the Seminole Indians, conditions were not much better than for the Freedmen. For Chief Coacoochee's band of Seminole, or for the Seminoles in general. Life was difficult as the reservation was poor in game and was much colder than the climate they were used to. Though federal government authorities expected them to farm, the lands were infertile and subject to drought. The Seminoles soon were dependent on agency handouts and some were starving.

In 1848 Principal Chief Micanopy passed away and as Micanopy's sister's son, Coacoochee was the next in line in the matrilineal tradition of the tribe to inherit the important leadership position. When the Seminole National Council passed him over for Chief Jumper, a proslavery, pro-Creek who was close to the Indian Sub-Agent Marcellus Duvall, a known trafficker in slaves and enemy of Horse's black Seminole. Coacoochee and John Horse had finally had enough. They soon led a combined party from Wewoka, and the Indian Territory under cover of night. The party involved more than a hundred black Seminole with as many fleeing Seminole Indians, and in the months to come the group would be pursued, raided, harassed and hounded nonstop. Heading south across the Red River into Texas, a journey that would take them nearly a year, the group struggled towards Mexico.

An agreement Seminole Chief Coacoochee had negotiated with representatives of the Mexican government to grant his group land on which to settle in Mexico in remuneration for his services of stopping raids and intrusions by Texas whites and Comanche raiders, was the hope the group looked to as they moved through drier and increasingly dangerous country. Throughout the fall of 1849 and into the summer of 1850, John Horse and Chief Coacoochee led the group towards the southern frontier, taking aboard a group of Kickapoo Indians along the way. It was a disappointment to the Texans when the group of Rangers and their allies arrived to see the Seminole Indians and their black Seminole compatriots as well as the Kickapoo who had joined them crossing the river. They soon met with officials in the Mexican state of Coahuila and in exchange for a promise to repel raiding white and

SEMINOLE

Indian parties from Texas, the Seminole refugees were granted land for their people and the group's leaders received captaincies in the Mexican army on or about July 12, 1850.

Known in Mexico as "Mascogos", the Mexicans in 1852 gave the Mascogo of John Horse and the Seminole Indians under Coacoochee, as well as the band of Southern Kickapoos who had allied with them on the trek separate land grants at Nacimiento to establish military colonies. With land, tools, and livestock provided to start their new lives in Mexico, these immigrants were able to focus on their role in the area, primarily to fight against Apache and Comanche raiders, and assist in repelling Anglo Texan incursions as well. The Mexican officials dealt solely with John Horse as the undisputed leader of the Mascogo people, and referred to him as El Capitán Juan Caballo in correspondence from the time.

In Mexico, the Black Seminoles established new communities and worked protecting their adopted country from attacks by slave raiders. When slavery finally ended in the United States, Black Seminoles were tempted to leave Mexico. In 1870 the U.S. government offered them money and land to return to the United States and work as scouts for the army. Many did return and serve as scouts, but the government never made good on its promise of land and support. In addition to standard pay for their services the federal government agreed to provide the black Seminole scouts with rations for their families, agricultural equipment, livestock and compensation for their relocation to permanent land grants. No physical copy of this agreement has been found, but it is very clear that many promises were made to the Black Seminoles that were never kept.

Renty Grayson, a Black Seminole scout, exemplary service in the Palo Dura Canyon Battle which took place Sept. 22, 1874[37].

The black Seminole "Mascogos" crossed the border from Mexico into Texas on July 4 and were officially mustered into military service on August 18 at Fort Duncan, near Eagle Pass, Texas, having joined the U.S. Army as a new unit known as the

---

[37] Schomburg Center for Research in Black Culture, Photographs and Prints Division, The New York Public Library. "Renty Grayson, a Black Seminole scout." The New York Public Library Digital Collections. [187-?]-[197-] - 1910. http://digitalcollections.nypl.org/items/510d47e2-ed39-a3d9-e040-e00a18064a99

SEMINOLE

"Seminole Negro Indian Scouts". In July 1872, most of the black Seminole Indian scouts were moved to Fort Clark, near Brackettville Texas. These Black Seminole Scouts, who were employed by the U.S. Army between 1870 and 1914 have a history of exemplary service. Because most of the Seminole scouts were of African ancestry, they were often attached to the Buffalo Soldier regiments, to guide the troops through hostile territory. The greatest portion of their service was in the 1870s when they played a major role in ending the Texas-Indian Wars.

John Horse himself though never served with these scouts although many of his tribesmen did. An assassination attempt targeting him by white Texans provoked John Horse to once again lead some of the Mascogos back into Mexico. He died there in 1882 while on a mission to represent them before Mexican president Porfirio Diaz (Littlefield, 2001). For several generations the Texas black Seminole served as guides and scouts admirably, but lacking ties to the larger body of Indians in Indian Territory were left behind and lost their group status as officially part of the "Seminole". By 1881, Texas had been in part thanks to the black Seminole secured for settlers and the role they had played was ending with that of the frontier. They were simply no longer needed for their skills developed over generations as warriors. The Black Seminole in Texas were never given land in Indian Territory as promised.

Many of them lived in poverty with some of the original scouts passing away paupers as the 20th century dawned on a community shrinking and on hard times. The numbers of black Seminole serving as scouts enlisted in the service steadily diminished, and in 1914 the scouts were officially disbanded. With the official end of their use, the 207 Black Seminole whose homes were at Fort Clark, TX were evicted from their homes, with only a handful of the oldest elderly who had served so loyally permitted to stay.

The Black Seminoles still in the area were split over trying to return to the Seminole Nation or returning to Nacimiento across the border in Mexico. In the end the group split up as some returned to Nacimiento while others found refuge with Seminole freedman relatives living in communities in the Seminole Nation.

Others continued to remain in the vicinity of Fort Clark while some moved to nearby Brackettville, where the Seminole Indian Scout Cemetery is located. Here many of the scouts are buried together in Kinney County, Texas, including Medal of Honor recipients, John Ward, Pompey Factor, Adam Paine and Isaac Payne. After four and a half decades of loyal service and untold danger and struggle, the black Seminole scouts and their community would be left with nothing more than memories of days gone by and the sound of broken promise echoing in their future, and scattered to refuge where they could find it.

Today their descendants still gather and all are proud of their heritage as a unique people, yet few if any in Texas hold status as Native American or have Seminole citizenship. Reunions and cultural celebrations are held on a regular basis by Black Seminole descendants from all three communities, and despite their modern differences, Black Seminole descendants in Texas, Oklahoma, and Mexico take great pride in their common heritage. The question of their status that has racked their cousins among the Creek and Seminole nations does not trouble the descendants of those who moved to Texas. They are not part of the federal Indian system anymore, no longer have a difference between themselves and other tribal members to be concerned with. They are now a distinct ethnicity within the many that call Texas home, and see their modern identity as such rather than as a tribal people struggling to maintain that status.

SEMINOLE

Black Seminole "Mascogos" Left to right: Plenty Payne, Billy July, Ben July, Dembo Factor (civilian clothes), Ben Wilson (back row), John July, William Shields; John Jefferson, Informant, January 1889[38].

---

[38] Schomburg Center for Research in Black Culture, Photographs and Prints Division, The New York Public Library. "Left to right : Plenty Payne, Billy July, Ben July, Dembo Factor (civilian clothes), Ben Wilson (back row), John July, William Shields; John Jefferson, Informant, January 1889." The New York Public Library Digital Collections. 1889.
http://digitalcollections.nypl.org/items/510d47dc-501f-a3d9-e040-e00a18064a99

The tale of John Horse's life and that of his band of "Mascogo", black Seminole, reflects the deep ties all the several black Seminole groups from Mexico, Oklahoma, Florida, and the Bahamas all have to their history as active participants in preserving their own freedom and seeking to preserve their unique identity whatever the costs. The example of men like black Seminole leader John Horse, the Seminole Negro Indian Scouts and Medal of Honor recipients John Ward, Pompey Factor, Adam Paine and Isaac Payne, and all black Seminole who fought fiercely to maintain the legacy of their freedom is today a testament to their strength and courage.

DISENROLLMENT

The struggle by the Freedmen of Cherokee and Seminole Nations to retain their citizenship in their tribes is just a part of a larger phenomenon underway with the arrival of the 21st century; tribes removing enrolled members from their rolls, a troubling trend called *"the ultimate goal of colonialist extinction by paperwork"* in one critics words. There has been increasing attempts to disenroll tribal members across the country in recent years for several reasons, from political posturing to disputes of ancestral ties. Indian Country had been awakening to this disturbing trend. To draw attention to the issue and to stop disenrollment in tribal communities several activists, artists and at least one elected tribal leader joined a prominent coalition of campaigners to raise awareness, in 2016, a movement that joined a growing chorus of calls for arbitrary disenrollment to be confronted and addressed.

Over eighty tribes have removed members from their rolls in recent years according to the groups assertions. *"As many as 10,000 people have lost their membership in what has been called a nationwide epidemic"*, reports one source, and attention to the alarming situation has grown. Indian community leaders like Winona LaDuke, and Greg Sarris, the chairman of the Federated Indians of Graton Rancheria in California, are seeking to end the controversial practice that is becoming all too common. The movement is asking Indian people all over the country to share on their social media platforms, why the practice of disenrolling tribal members over political struggles can harm Indian Country, sovereignty, and all native peoples.

"Cowardly self-extinction," said Gary Davis in a 2016 interview[39]. Davis, the president and CEO of the National Center for American Indian Enterprise Development. The Cherokee Nation, with whom he is an enrolled member, has weathered criticism for its attempts to deny tribal citizenship to thousands of Freedmen, an effort in which we have seen in this work it was largely unsuccessful. Disenrollment has long been an issue though largely

---

[39] https://www.indianz.com/News/2016/02/09/national-campaign-launched-to.asp

unaddressed, but is currently getting more coverage as it is increasingly used as a political football, viewed as dangerous to foundational established relationships of tribal sovereignty; Not a new phenomenon in Indian Country by any means, it hasn't always been a weapon of political posturing but has at times been related to traditional tribal cultures clashing with mainstream expectations of governance, or as a result of the modern political realities of tribal nations.

In 1978, Santa Clara Pueblo v. Martinez was an important U.S. Supreme Court decision, one that's impacts are still felt and oft debated even today. The case arose when the Pueblo officials upheld a tribal law that disallowed enrollment of children born to women who marry outside of the tribe. Most controversial was the fact that in the culture of the Pueblo, children of males who do the same were not denied membership. The decision from the court was an important one. Santa Clara Pueblo v. Martinez was a case that shaped issues of tribal sovereignty today accepted as standard; tribes determine their own membership.

Disenrollment as a phenomenon though has garnered increasing attention in the last couple decades as the episodes of disenrollment have been tenuously if at all connected to the exercise of tribal sovereignty, and in the view of some clearly arbitrary and politically motivated. As foundational to the tribal-federal relationship, tribal governments have not relinquished their inherent right to establish and dictate their own membership criteria, yet an increasing number of legal scholars and community advocates point out that there are many cases of tribal members having revoked their official inclusion as members of their communities, often for seemingly arbitrary reasons. The critics as well also complain that some tribal resolution procedures do not offer adequate protections for people who are being removed.

In 2015 the National Native American Bar Association acted to address the disenrollment issue with the presentation of a resolution and ethics opinion. The group would adopt Resolution #2015-06, *"Supporting Equal Protection and Due Process for Any Divestment of the American Indigenous Right of Tribal Citizenship."* The position the NNABA took was one which denounced the political or arbitrary disenrolling of tribal members, stating it was "immoral and unethical" for "any lawyer" to help tribal governments disenroll tribal members without allowing for adequate process for redressing the rights of the those affected. NNABA's actions was the first time that any of the several national Indian organizations had addressed head-on the issue of growing disenrollment controversies. Legal advocates and attorneys in the realm of tribal law often wait for Native American leaders to lead on issues of national Indian policy, but the NNABA felt that tribal leadership were to slow to address the disenrollment epidemic and so acted.

The efforts of those seeking to draw attention to disenrollment issues may be working; in some parts of Indian Country including in the councils of the Federated Indians of Graton Rancheria, the Spokane Tribe of Washington and the Passamaquoddy Tribe at Pleasant Point in Maine, tribal governments have recently amended their legal frameworks to make it more difficult to remove members from the tribal roll. Such efforts are good since beyond tribal court systems and other tribally sanctioned resolution processes, those who are disenrolled have recourse to few external authorities to seek redress of complaints concerning the tribal governments membership decisions. Due to tribal sovereignty occupying a central and foundational place in Indian Country, most federal courts shy away from controversial cases of disenrollment, and the Bureau of Indian Affairs often has a hands off attitude as well except in the most extreme cases, as with that of the Seminole Nation and Cherokee Nation concerning the Freedmen.

On a rare occasion, Congressional legislators have been known to wade into the fray though, such as when the 2008 Native American Housing Assistance and Self Determination Act authorization was used as a tool to disallow the Cherokee Nation from sharing in the federal housing funding it needed if the Cherokee National Council continued its efforts to remove from the roll the Freedmen, while litigation concerning the issue worked its way through the courts. The Eastern Band of Cherokee Indians in North Carolina considered the adoption of stronger laws for the prosecution of tribal members who are convicted of dealing drugs, even debating in 2015 a resolution that could lead to banishment or disenrollment. Joseph Hamilton, the chairman of the Ramona Band of Cahuilla Indians, challenged national tribal leaders, governments, and organizations to confront the disenrollment epidemic sweeping Indian Country, as has several other tribal leaders.

> *In Southern California, where my tribe calls home, disenrollment is common, in part because of big gaming revenues and internal power struggles. It is also a symptom of the breakdown of traditional tribal power structures. Simply put, some tribal leaders listen to lawyers instead of elders.*

The Saginaw Chippewa Tribe of Michigan in 2015 as well reopened disenrollment proceedings against more than 230 people, including some who are deceased, after the tribe's appeals court agreed for the cases to be heard again even though some of those facing removal thought the matter was closed. Possibly most shocking of the recent spate of disenrollment was removal of the descendants of a chief who was put to death a century and a half ago and barely a year after he signed a key treaty, with the decision that they can be removed from the Confederated Tribes of Grand Ronde in Oregon, a judge ruled recently. Chief Tumulth joined the 1855 Willamette Valley Treaty that promised a reservation for the confederated tribes, yet since his family didn't move there before or after he was "wrongly executed" in 1856, those who count him among their ancestors are ineligible for membership, Confederated Tribes of Grand Ronde Judge David Shaw determined.

The ruling meant the Confederated Tribes of Grand Ronde tribal government can now remove 86 of Chief Tumulth's descendants from the rolls, who are unable to demonstrate ties to a base roll that was created in 1872 subsequent to the chiefs' execution by the Army for allegedly participating in an "Indian uprising". The late Ida Altringer, who served as elder grand marshal for the Confederated Tribes of Grand Ronde passed on in 2008, but after her death, the tribe's enrollment committee disenrolled her, drawing the ire from many across Indian Country. family

DISENROLLMENT

spokesperson Mia Prickett put the tribe's actions into perspective from the family's point of view.

> *"Ironically this activist judge used the U.S. Army's execution of my grandfather to justify his termination of my tribal status today, speaking of execution, that's exactly what happened to my family. Even our deceased relatives were terminated and it is disgusting."*

In some corners the opinion is that the use of separating those unappreciative of their tribal status is of understandable benefit to the tribe. The year 2015 would see a surge in threats of disenrollment as well as resistance to its use, as well as talk of other means of establishing order in communities over whelmed with addiction and violence. Several tribes, including the Standing Rock Sioux Tribe of South Dakota, Spirit Lake Tribe of North Dakota, and Blackfeet Tribe of Montana, considered using the ancient practice of "tribal banishment" to deal with their own enrolled member's drug dealing on their tribal lands. Such banishment is in contrast to disenrollment though, when a tribal citizen is permanently removed from the tribal community and such actions often lack consensus in the wider Indian community.

After consideration most of the above mentioned tribes did not accept disenrollment as a punishment of tribal members for drug dealing crimes, but the Cheyenne River Sioux Tribe decided to not only banish for life, but to disenroll tribal citizens convicted of dealing drugs on sovereign tribal lands on their reservation. The move was highly controversial to say the least. As one commentator said *"it seems that Cheyenne River has resorted to colonial—rather than traditional Lakota—penal modes"*. But as political scientist Louis Henkin pointed out arbitrary and political usage of disenrollment is harmful to tribal sovereign status as "dependent domestic nations" with a unique government to government relationship with the federal government.

> *"sovereignty as a right to do as one pleases is part of the concept, but not sovereignty as anarchy, not*

> *sovereignty as resistance to cooperation. And not sovereignty as immunity."*

The Indian social media world as well as native academics have responded to the disenrollment crises not only during the Oklahoma Freedmen controversies but in many of the increasingly common episodes of disenrollment. Professor David E. Wilkins, a member of the Lumbee Tribe of Cheraw Indians in North Carolina, discussed the dangers of disenrollment to future generations in Indian Country, a slippery slope of uncertain outcomes. He sees the legacy created by the Bureau of Indian Affairs and other federal agencies and departments as they imposed regulations and policies designed to reduce the number of Native citizens deemed "eligible" for federal or even treaty-based benefits at the root of the current disenrollment crises.

> *"This disenrollment occurs for a number of reasons. Some, such as fraudulent enrollment, dual membership, or failure to maintain contact with the home community are arguably legitimate; others, however, are fundamentally tainted and bear the mark of rank injustice—political power plays, economic greed, and pseudo-scientific arguments about insufficient blood quantum, among others."*

Whatever the ultimate outcome of the current struggles over disenrollment are, the appearance of such politicized controversies should lead all tribal people to deeply evaluate the established relationship of their selves to their tribal community and government, and of that to the larger state and federal governments with which they interact. The identity of Native Americans and of the future of tribal languages, cultures, and communities are deeply held legacies that should not be wantonly endangered for political gain or passing benefit by individuals or groups at harm to the entirety of Indian Country. There has long been resistance to the parameters of the "tribal sovereignty" model that has governed Indian and tribal community life. In his "Longest Walk" speech in Washington DC in 1977, Phillip Deere, a revered Muscogee Creek elder who was active in the American Indian Movement and who took part in many national native rights activities and international

DISENROLLMENT

conferences and forums on indigenous issues voiced a disconnect between tribal member and authentic tribal governance that is now even more pronounced four decades later.

> *"When my Indian people were no longer acting like Indians and they were no longer thinking like Indians... I refused to go to any organizations within my own tribe, or any other tribe. I refused to accept any government programs because none of their programs would bring my children home. None of them would ever make me more Indian. But it would take all the Indianness out of me. So I closed my doors and only looked after my family and my children[40]."*

Such is the feeling of many traditionally oriented Indians almost a half century later. Native American nations are generally unconstrained by the U.S. Constitution in the eyes of many, only bound to uphold provisions akin to those found in the Bill of Rights by statute, and even then the Supreme Court has ruled that tribal nations are not required to "apply or interpret civil rights protections directly in line with state and federal governments". Tribes use their inherent tribal sovereignty to preserve their differentness, even in such situations when tribal laws are seemingly in opposition to the American civil rights norms of mainstream society; this being the case then where is the leadership in asserting the egalitarian and collective values of tribal society as it stood for millennia?

The Freedmen controversies and disenrollment crises reveal a need for a critical and comprehensive examination of contemporary tribal governance, especially so considering the evolving international norms concerning good governance. Such changing paradigms as those underway in many parts of the globe increasingly lay out criteria of the commitments governments owe to their citizens, tribal or otherwise.

The emergence of increasing concerns and actions facilitating good governance within an evolving human rights landscape, one demanding humanitarian concerns and equality before the law for

---

[40] http://mvskokee.tripod.com/

all, suggests that indigenous nations should consider revising the conventional (western) ideas of good governance entertained in the recent past, and instead the implementing of good governance forms and practices rooted in indigenous identity and values. Such change doesn't necessarily demand that tribal nations entirely diverge from or adhere to those of modern western democracy. Instead if tribal nations give Native American principles of government derived more from tribally oriented cultural and traditional perspectives a chance, approaches which facilitate the evolution of newer forms of tribal governance that restore functionality and support justice, harmony, and inclusiveness in tribal communities, gains in quality of life measures may be made. Good governance by tribes through native based cultural practices may well better enable tribal nations to facilitate improved self-governance, protect better the sovereign status for all tribes, and ensure their continued and strengthened cultural and political existence.

CONCLUSION

What does the struggles of the Freedmen of the Five Tribes tell us about Indian Country and the Native American identity today? Without doubt there is greater economic and political opportunity than ever for Native Americans as individuals and groups, even as there is a growing dialogue of some questioning the relationship between the federal government and the tribes and the limits of sovereignty. Taiaiake Alfred (Mohawk) wrote in the preface to his second edition *of Peace, Power, and Righteousness: An Indigenous Manifesto*:

> *"I came to learn and appreciate the views of those Native people who looked critically at what was being achieved through 'Aboriginal self-government' or 'tribal sovereignty' and saw the movement as vacuous and devoid of indigenous culture or any spiritual connection to ancestral teachings. In this view, Natives gaining control of governing structures is not enough to allow us to decolonize. In fact, without a cultural grounding, self-government becomes a kind of Trojan horse for capitalism, consumerism, and selfish individualism."*

Seeing tribal communities who survived colonial settlement, the Removal, the Civil War, The Great Depression, the Dawes Allotment Act, and the rigors of modernity allowing casino money or political posturing by tribal politicos to erode the integrity as governments and sovereign peoples is saddening to many observers across Indian Country. My friend Cedric Sunray is a MOWA Choctaw, whose family is from a tribal community much like my own "Dominicker" Dead Lakes people of historic Scotts Ferry, Florida. He is an educator in the Oklahoma Public Schools and participated greatly in contributing to the dialogue concerning such issues as disenrollment, and especially the role "blood quantum" plays in the current drive towards select racialized definitions of indigenous identity, and relevance to Indian Country in general.

> *"The blood quantum issue is even more irrelevant. There are many tribes here in Oklahoma who herald their "inclusiveness" due to their lineal descendant requirement as opposed to strict blood quantum standards. Some of these tribes, for instance, attempted to use this supposed "inclusivity" as proof that they have no prejudice during their attempted removals of the Indian Freedmen population."*

The story of the Creek, Seminole, and especially Cherokee Nation Freedmen's struggle for political inclusion are examples of the fraught balancing act of civil rights as Americans versus the collective tribal sovereignty of indigenous nations. That these two important aspects of the unique political identity experienced by Native Americans can at times be antithetical of the other and in some instances divisive, is a subject that needs more attention, as is well illustrated in the playing out of the Freedmen controversies, or the growing incidents of disenrollment that have been occurring across Indian Country.

As Americans the civil rights enjoyed by all are applicable to each citizen in equal measure, and ideally mean the protection of every individual's equality and an expected participation in the national narrative of the times. The exercising of the sovereign power of federally recognized tribal governments includes groups collective rights as a tribe and as well intentional actions taken from the reserved and autonomous political identity of that tribe on behalf of its citizens. The rights that Americans hold as citizens are viewed by many as oppositional to racial discrimination, whereas sovereign rights are associated less with race and racism and more with the unique political status of indigenous peoples as citizens of domestic dependent nations.

Sovereignty implies that Indian tribes as "dependent nations" are not minorities, and in light of the ongoing narrative on indigenous sovereignty and its limits revealed by the Freedmen's struggle for inclusion, truly more relevant than ever, even as American Indian

CONCLUSION

as a political category is increasingly obscured as the tropes of race based struggle and calls for social equality becoming louder on the social and political scene. This is especially prescient in light of exponentially increasing racial diversity of enrolled tribal members in many tribes. Native peoples have very different ideas of individual and communal identity than that have become established from the American experiment in the triumph of civil rights, and the reconciliation of the two must by nature be an ongoing effort.

As one researcher said, *"issues of indigenous politics are inadequately addressed by either civil rights discourse or pluralist discourses of inclusion, even while they are misconstrued as [being] race based.* (Kauanui, 2008)". The assertion that tribal sovereignty as federally construed is something solely political without significant racial implications is not supported by history, even as a focusing on the civil rights of individuals in Indian Country can restrict understandings of historic native political processes; neither civil rights nor tribal sovereignty can be addressed in overly racial terms, as neither can be ignored.

Like the twin brothers who are culture heroes found among many tribes of the southeast, race and (indigenous) political identities have long been intimately linked yet in struggle in Indian Country, as in America in general. The revoking of tribally held identities has increased on several fronts in recent years as we have seen. The spate of disenrollment controversies wracking some tribal communities of late reflect an alarming shared interest between the non-Indian governments and the tribal sovereigns, one in no way of obvious benefit to the indigenous identity.

> *"The incidence of disenrollment which is now occurring in Indian Country is uncontrollable. Of the more than 60 tribes who have disenrolled their tribal members in the last 20 years, there exists a significantly larger number who have done so outside of the watchful eye of news reporters and even more who have now enshrined disenrollment justification language in their own tribal constitutions."*

The Freedmen's Quandary

As the above perspective shared by Cedric Sunray shows, one must think, if this is what we know, imagine that which we don't. The struggles for inclusion of the Freedmen are in some ways a 'canary in the coal mine' type scenario, as are the increasing cases of disenrollment among tribes. Racialization of Native American tribal identity and unchecked economic greed are driving disenrollment efforts even as tribal governments are increasingly falling prey to both, though these actions are clearly antithetical to long time Native American tribal values.

Lost in the arguments and counter-arguments of the Freedmen controversy are the stakes the Cherokee people, as well as the United States, has in the results. America's "Indian problem" has haunted it across the more than 200 years of its history. Some native activists see assimilation of the surviving indigenous population as an ultimate result and for native persons cut off from tribal relations, assimilation is the only recourse, and long viewed as the true goal of the non-native governments of North America by critics. Indian Country Media Networks's Opinions Page Editor Ray Cook recently commented on a growing sentiment among some in Indian Country that a line must be drawn, that the balancing act is unsustainable.

> *"I am not big on the capitulations the Cherokee and their sister nations have made over the decades. What self-respecting nation would even consider allowing the BIA to have final approval on their government amendments and referendums? The IRA is killing our understanding of sovereignty ...Political assimilation is no different than cultural assimilation. If a Native leader claims to be a proud American, I applaud them and their convictions. And we all should help them move their belongings so they can live among them."*

For the Cherokee Nation of Oklahoma, now a tribe of over 300,000 members of whom most are physically or culturally indistinguishable from their non-native neighbors, the judge's decision to include the Freedmen as tribal citizens despite some having no Indian ancestry is an acknowledgment of a bridge to a future identity very different to the ancient "racially American

CONCLUSION

Indian" Cherokee government of five centuries ago but evolved steadily since contact through to the present. The identity dissonance between the "political" Native American" and the "racial" American Indian may soon have to be reconciled across Indian Country. With diminishing federal resources and funding, racially Indian majority tribes and those of little Indian ancestry for the average enrolled citizen like the Cherokee Nation of Oklahoma (and many other eastern tribes) will likely come into increasing conflict over the meaning of native identity.

With little outside access to the actual average degree of Indian blood of Indian tribal members, these fissures are continuing to invisibly deepen behind the "Buckskin Curtain" of Indian Country. The "racial" diversification of individuals included in the populace of Indian Country will have an increasingly significant effect on the perceptions of Native American identity by outsiders, but what will this mean for the place of Indian sovereignty in the federal framework in the long run?

Most certainly to attempt to simplify a complex racial environment as the Cherokee Nation at the turn of the twentieth century into broad categories such as "Cherokee by blood" or "Freedmen" and employ them as if those are accurate is to do a disservice to the history and present dignity of the Cherokee Nation and Indian Country overall; to continue to make legal use of such a record known to be so arbitrary as a basis for enrollment by a modern tribal people in the 21st century is to accept wholeheartedly the colonization of one's own political process, according to the view of several anti-colonial Native American activists I spoke to. The Creek and Seminole Freedmen are facing many of the same challenges as those among the Cherokee, as well as difficulties unique to the history of each nation. All share the issue of the clash of "Indian blood" and nationhood, and individual rights versus collective rights.

The reality is that non-indigenous perceptions of blood are still the primary determiner, whether they mandate blood quantum or not; this can marginalize or eliminate adopted children who are reared in the tribal community, long-time intermarried non-native spouses who have been socially included in the community for many years and who have children, grandchildren, and even great-grandchildren who are part of the community, members of other Indian tribes and their descendants who found refuge in other Indian communities in generations past, those from the tribe whose mothers are members when the tribe requires patrilineal descent or those from the community but born of a tribal man when the enrolled membership criteria require matrilineal descent.

Non-native perceptions of blood as a primary determiner of the identity can disenfranchise children raised in the community who are the biological offspring of an intermarried individual who had married or partnered into the tribe after their birth, Freedmen descendants who either accurately or erroneously were placed on rolls not delineating blood, yet whose ancestors slaved in the fields for years of those who were, and other individuals who have become culturally and socially integrated into the community over the years, but do not share the same biological ties or DNA with those who claim them as fellow tribal community members.

Money has come to play a major role in the definitions of tribal inclusion in the 21st century, though this is hardly new, only increasingly prevalent. I will present one example from my own family as illustrative. Even while the battle for the benefits of recognition or inclusion as a member of a tribe is not new, Native American entrepreneurship based on that recognition goes back generations in the Creek Nation. By a treaty of March 24, 1832, the Creeks were forced into ceding to the United States all of their land east of the Mississippi River, and the heads of families were entitled to tracts of land which were to include their improvements.

In 1833 Benjamin S. Parsons and Thomas J. Abbott prepared a census of the heads of families among the Upper and Lower Towns of the Creek Nation, in anticipation of the removal of the Creeks to the west. As a descendent of Nimrod Doyle, who was enumerated on this tribal roll as a citizen of Broken Arrow Tribal Town, a non-Indian who inserted himself into Creek Nation politics, economy, and ultimately removal land dealings, he used his tribal membership to garner personal gain, as did many Indian Countryman and mixed blood elites. Illustrative of this was an inclusion in the Creek Treaty of 1805 granting Creeks exclusivity

CONCLUSION

in the operation of "stations" along a federal road from Ocmulgee, Georgia to Mobile, Alabama.

These ferries and "houses of entertainment" were lucrative as the new federal road passed through parts of Creek Nation, over lands purchased as an easement (Bowen, 2000), and Doyle like dozens of others operated such a station near Pole Cat Springs. As I explored in ***The Belles of the Creek Nation***, Doyle was a non-native "Indian Countryman" with two Creek wives from leading families from two different tribal towns (Koweta and Kasita), and he utilized those connections for personal gain. Some would say that a clear path to ruin of the nation itself can be seen in the steady assimilation of the creek tribal people into the non-egalitarian values of the Americans, with slavery and personal enrichment by the leadership signs of the coming ruination and removal of the Creek Nation. While this is arguable on the one hand, the lessons of history when not heeded are repeated.

Even at that early date, and seemingly as a balance to the growing erosion of egalitarian tribal identity among the Creeks as slavery and capitalist ideas became more established among the mixed blood elites, there were some "free blacks" listed within the Parson Abbot census, a total of 11 as heads of household with one referred to by name as the husband of an Indian woman. As well there were many enslaved people who gained their freedom from their Creek owners; once their freedom was obtained, these fortunate ones often received citizenship within the Creek Nation and several are listed by name.

A Kaw elder I used to attend sweat lodge with in Pawhuska, Oklahoma used to say that before the arrival of the Europeans, Indians didn't know that we were Indians with a laugh. The steady force of non-native culture in shaping and influence that of Indian communities and identity is significant, including views of inclusion in the Indian community. Few tribal members who don't speak their language or follow a very traditional lifeway even perceive this. The colonial mindset is especially string among eastern tribes. In a nutshell, this colonial mentality is built up over the centuries of narratives and legal fictions that presented American Indians (and people of color in general) as inferior people compared to white settlers who were supposedly racially and culturally superior.

In 2006, when the Judicial Appeals Tribunal of the Cherokee Nation recognized that Lucy Allen and fellow Cherokee Freedmen, descendants of African slaves once owned by Cherokee, are entitled to citizenship in the Cherokee Nation and had been citizens of the Cherokee Nation since the 1866 treaty with the United States. When in less than a year, the Cherokee Nation subsequently amended its constitutional criteria to restrict citizenship to descendants of those listed on the Dawes Roll as Cherokee, Delaware or Shawnee Indian by blood, and in effect revoking the citizenship of all 2,800 citizens who are legally solely Cherokee Freedmen descendants, the issues raised and later resolved will undoubtedly resound for years.

The Oklahoma and national news headlines in late 2017 reporting that the two views of Cherokee peoplehood, one political and the other race based and held by communities involved in the decades long struggle were intent on "linking arms (and) marching forward" signaled that as this chapter of the struggle for belonging ended another began in the ongoing narrative of belonging and identity in Indian country. Uncontested acceptance of the final decision on Freedmen citizenship was part of an important and ongoing evolution of the relationship between the diverse people of the Cherokee Nation. Having looked in greater detail at the struggles by the Freedmen of the Five Tribes for inclusion facilitates a better understand of the not-to-distant future as the racial diversity of tribes increases and the role of Indian Country in the American experiment continues to evolve. The crossroads of identity that the Creek, Seminole, and Cherokee Nations, as well as Indian Country as a whole, once again finds themselves at in the 21st century is central to issues of individual and tribal sovereignty, and reflective of larger questions of race and identity that American must address.

Index

Abraham, Black Seminole, 69
African Americans percent of Indian ancestry on average, 9
Alabama (tribe), 41, 82, 106
Alfred, Taiaiake, 101
all-black towns in Oklahoma, 51
Allen, Lucy, 107
Altringer, Ida, 96
American Indian Movement, ii, ix, 23, 98
American Indian Religious Freedom Act of 1978, 17
American Isolate, xi
Apache people, 87
Apalachicola people, 82
Arbeka OK, 47
Baker, Bill John, 36
Barnet, Toney, 85
black Cherokee, xiv, 35
Black Seminole, vii, 43, 58, 59, 63, 65, 68, 70, 72, 73, 74, 80, 82, 85, 88, 89, 90, 91
Blackfeet Tribe of Montana, 97
blood quantum, vi, vii, xii, xiv, xix, 14, 29, 30, 44, 56, 57, 58, 60, 65, 66, 67, 73, 76, 80, 98, 101, 102, 105
Bluebird, Ronnie, 23
Brackettville TX, 75, 89, 90
Braggs, OK, 34
Broken Arrow Tribal Town, 106
Browne, Erin, 2
Bruner, Paro, 42
Buckskin Curtain, 105
Buffalo Soldiers, 89
Bureau of Indian Affairs, 16, 29, 39, 58, 60, 65, 66, 73, 77, 78, 79, 95, 98
Burgess, Sharon, 70
By Blood Rolls, xiv, 10, 28, 36, 44, 45
Byrd, Joe, 22, 23
Caribbean, 3, 59
Catawba people, 20
Certificate Degreeof Indian Blood (CDIB), 9
Cheraw people, 20, 98
Cherokee Marshals, 22
Cherokee Nation, ii, iv, vi, vii, xii, xiii, xiv, xv, xix, xxiii, xxiv, 1, 4, 5, 7, 8, 9, 10, 14, 19, 20, 21, 22, 23, 24, 25, 26, 27, 28, 29, 30, 31, 33, 34, 35, 36, 48, 60, 61, 93, 95, 102, 104, 105, 107, 108
Cherokee Nation v. Georgia (1831), xxiii, 36
Cherokee Nation v. Nash, 25, 36
Cherokee National Council, 21, 22, 95

Index

Cherokee National Historical Society, xviii

Cherokee Old Settlers. *See* Keetoowah Cherokee

Cheyenne River Sioux Tribe, 97

Cheyenne-Arapaho Tribe of OK, xii

Chickasaw Freedmen, 39

Chickasaw Nation, iii, xv, xvi, 2, 7, 8, 11, 13, 39, 40, 61

Chief Tumulth, 96

Choctaw Freedmen, 39

Choctaw Nation, iii, xiv, xvi, 2, 5, 7, 8, 11, 13, 21, 29, 39, 40, 61, 101

Christie, Chooch, 23

Chupco, Sally, 73

citizenship, ii, vi, vii, xiii, xiv, xv, xvi, xix, xx, xxiv, 9, 11, 12, 15, 24, 25, 26, 27, 28, 29, 30, 31, 34, 35, 39, 43, 44, 45, 46, 47, 48, 52, 53, 55, 58, 60, 61, 62, 65, 66, 68, 70, 80, 90, 93, 107, 108

Civil Rights Act of 1968, xxi, 30

Civil War, iv, vi, xv, 7, 8, 9, 27, 36, 39, 40, 42, 43, 49, 62, 65, 67, 71, 78, 83, 101

Coacoochee, 81, 83, 85, 86, 87

Comanche people, 7, 86, 87

Confederate States of America, 7, 8

Confederated Tribes of Grand Ronde, 96

Congress, v, xv, 11, 12, 77, 78

Cook, Ray, 104

Cooper, Kenneth, 31

Creek Nation, i, iii, viii, xiv, xvi, xviii, 2, 5, 6, 7, 8, 9, 11, 13, 20, 21, 24, 27, 39, 40, 41, 42, 43, 44, 45, 46, 47, 48, 49, 50, 51, 52, 53, 55, 61, 62, 63, 73, 76, 80, 81, 82, 83, 84, 85, 86, 90, 98, 102, 105, 106, 107, 108

Creek Nation population 2018, 44

Cunningham, Mary Ann, 53

Daily Oklahoman newspaper, 25

Davis, Gary, 93

Dawes Roll, vii, xiv, xv, xvi, xvii, xviii, xix, xx, 6, 8, 9, 10, 11, 12, 13, 14, 15, 25, 27, 28, 42, 44, 45, 46, 47, 48, 53, 55, 57, 60, 61, 62, 63, 66, 70, 72, 76, 101, 108

Debo, Angie, 14, 15

Deere, Phillip, 98

Delaware Agreement of 1867, 28

Delaware people, 7, 28, 108

Department of the Interior, vii, 14, 16, 27, 40, 58, 67, 77, 78, 79
dependent domestic nations, xiii, xx, xxi, xxiv, 36, 86, 97, 102
Descendants of Freedmen of the Five Civilized Tribes, viii, 25, 31
Diaz, Porfirio, 89
disenrollment controversies, 57, 60, 93, 94, 95, 96, 97, 98, 99, 101, 102, 103, 104
DNA, i, 7, 10, 106
Dominickers, xii, 101
Doyle, Nimrod, 106, 107
Eagle Pass TX, 63, 88
Eastern Band of Cherokee Indians, 95
Euchee people, 22, 23, 82
Federal Census, iii, viii, 10, 56, 76, 106, 107
federally recognized tribes, v, xiii, 23, 29, 34, 67, 73, 75, 102
Fitzpatrick, Ellen, 14
Five (Civilized) Tribes, ii, iii, iv, v, vii, xvi, xvii, xx, xxiv, 1, 2, 5, 6, 7, 8, 9, 11, 13, 14, 27, 32, 39, 40, 43, 46, 47, 48, 52, 55, 56, 57, 60, 61, 82, 101, 108
Florida, i, vii, xii, 5, 6, 11, 23, 57, 58, 59, 60, 61, 62, 63, 64, 69, 71, 72, 73, 74, 75, 76, 77, 78, 81, 82, 83, 84, 92, 101
Fort Clark, TX, 89, 90
Fort Gibson OK, 21, 40, 84
Fort Pierce Reservation Seminole Tribe of Florida, 58, 73
Freedmen, v, iii, iv, v, vi, vii, xii, xiii, xiv, xv, xvii, xx, xxii, xxiii, xxiv, 4, 5, 7, 8, 9, 10, 11, 13, 24, 25, 26, 27, 28, 29, 30, 31, 32, 33, 34, 35, 36, 37, 39, 40, 42, 43, 45, 46, 48, 49, 50, 51, 52, 53, 55, 56, 57, 58, 59, 60, 61, 63, 64, 65, 66, 67, 68, 69, 70, 72, 73, 76, 78, 79, 80, 86, 93, 95, 98, 99, 101, 102, 103, 104, 105, 106, 108
Gallay, Alan, 2
Gates, Henry Louis Jr., 9, 80
General Allotment Act, xvi, 11, 45
General Jesup, 83, 84
Georgia, xxiii, 19, 36, 59, 82, 106
Graham, Blue, 47
Graton Rancheria, 93, 95
Grayson, Renty, 88
Gullah dialect, 74
Hair, Jesse, 34
Hamilton, Joseph, 96
Hancock, Ian, 74
Haney, Jerry, 65, 66, 78, 79

Index

Hill, S. Pony, 23
Hogan, Judge Thomas, 27, 35
Horse, John, 80, 81, 82, 83, 85, 86, 87, 89, 92
Indian Agent Duvall, 86
Indian Civil Rights Act, xxi
Indian Claims Commission, 64, 76, 78
Indian Country, v, ii, iv, viii, ix, xi, xii, xiii, xviii, xx, xxii, xxiv, 1, 11, 26, 28, 34, 56, 59, 60, 66, 71, 93, 94, 95, 96, 98, 101, 102, 103, 104, 105, 108
Indian Countryman, 106, 107
Indian New Deal, 15
Indian Reorganization Act (IRA), 13, 15, 16
Indian Self-Determination and Education Assistance Act, 16
Indian Territory, i, iii, iv, xiii, xv, xvi, xvii, 1, 5, 8, 9, 10, 11, 13, 14, 20, 21, 39, 40, 48, 51, 55, 58, 59, 62, 63, 67, 69, 71, 76, 78, 80, 81, 82, 83, 84, 85, 86, 89
Indian uprising, 96
intermarriage, vi, 43, 44, 63
Jack Brown Center, 23
Johnson, James Coody, 62
Kansas (state), viii, 1, 8
Kaskaskia people, 13
Kaw people, 107
Keetoowah Cherokee, xviii, xix, 12, 29
Kickapoo people, 86
LaDuke, Winona, 93
LeEtta Sampson, iii
Littlefield, Daniel F., 28, 40
Lumbee Tribe of Cheraw Indians, 98
Marilyn Vann, iii, vii, xxiv, 19, 21, 24, 25, 27, 31, 37, 60
Marilyn Vann's biographical sketch, 24
Mascogos, 87, 88, 89, 91
McCulley, Robert, 68
McKane, Jane, 66
Medal of Honor recipients, 90, 92
Mexican Army, 80
Mexico, 20, 21, 59, 60, 63, 74, 80, 86, 87, 88, 89, 90, 92
Miami people, 13
Micanopy, 86
Miccosukee Tribe, 72
mixed blood elite, 2, 4, 7, 10, 19, 24, 82, 106, 107
Mobile, AL, 106
Mulroy, Kevin, 59
Muscogee Creek Indian Freedmen Band, 39
Muscogee Nation Constitutional Convention of 1979, 45
Nacimiento de los Negros, Coahuila, Mexico, 75

National Native American Bar Association, 94
Native American Housing Assistance and Self Determination Act, 95
Nero, Roger, 30
New England, 2
Northeastern State University, 15
Ocmulgee, GA, 106
Oklahoma, ii, i, ii, iv, v, vi, vii, xi, xii, xiii, xiv, xv, xvii, xix, xx, 7, 9, 13, 15, 16, 17, 24, 26, 27, 29, 30, 34, 35, 36, 39, 43, 44, 47, 51, 52, 55, 57, 58, 59, 60, 61, 62, 63, 64, 65, 66, 67, 68, 70, 72, 74, 75, 76, 78, 79, 80, 81, 90, 92, 98, 101, 104, 107, 108
Oklahoma Indian Welfare Act of 1936, 16
Okmulgee OK, 47, 70
one drop rule, 43, 47, 61
Osage people, 7, 13
Osceola, 59, 83
Palo Dura Canyon Battle, 88
Pan-Indian, 17
Parson Abbot Roll of Creek Nation 1832, 107
Pawhuska, OK, 107
Peoria people, 13
Perryman, Grant, 45
Perryman, Leguest Choteau, 40
Piankeshaw people, 13

Ponca City OK, 24
Porter, Pleasant, 62
President Donald Trump, xiii
Prickett, Mia, 97
Quapaw people, 7
Quebec, 3
racial identity, iv, viii, xiii, xiv, xix, 10, 19, 28, 29, 30, 31, 32, 34, 35, 43, 44, 47, 51, 60, 77, 78, 102, 103, 104, 105, 108
racialized view of native identity, vi, 1, 2, 29, 36, 101
Ramona Band of Cahuilla Indians, 96
Redbird Smith, xix
Redbird Smith Ceremonial Grounds, xix, 23
Revolutionary War, 6
Rogers State University, xii, 24
Ron Graham, iii, 47
Rushforth, Brett, 2, 3
Russell Means, ii, ix, x
Sac and Fox Tribe of Oklahoma, xii
Saginaw Chippewa Tribe of Michigan, 96
Santa Clara Pueblo v. Martinez, 30, 94
Sarris, Greg, 93
Scots, 19
Scott family, v, ii, x, 20
Scott Momaday, ii, x
Scotts Ferry FL, 101

Index

Second Seminole War, 81, 84
Seminole Freedmen Bands, vii, 57, 67, 77
Seminole Land Claims Settlement 1970, 64
Seminole Nation, iii, vii, 5, 48, 52, 55, 56, 57, 58, 59, 60, 61, 62, 63, 64, 65, 66, 67, 68, 69, 70, 72, 74, 75, 76, 77, 78, 79, 80, 81, 82, 85, 89, 95
Seminole Negro Indian Scouts, 89, 92
Seminole people, vii, xiv, xvi, 2, 5, 6, 7, 8, 9, 11, 13, 20, 27, 32, 39, 40, 43, 46, 48, 52, 55, 56, 57, 58, 59, 60, 61, 62, 63, 64, 65, 66, 67, 68, 69, 70, 71, 72, 73, 74, 75, 76, 77, 78, 79, 80, 81, 82, 83, 84, 85, 86, 87, 88, 89, 90, 92, 93, 95, 102, 105, 108
Seminole Tribe of Florida, 58, 72, 73
Seneca people, 7
Sequoyah Research Center, 28
Shaw, Lena, 69, 96
Shawnee Agreement of 1869, 28
Shawnee Tribe of Oklahoma, xii, 28, 108
Simmons, Damario Solomon, 52

slave revolt of 1842 in Cherokee Nation, 20, 21
slavery, 3, 4, 5, 7, 19, 20, 21, 40, 41, 53, 71, 78, 80, 82, 83, 85, 87
Smith, Chad, 22, 23
Snyder, Christina, 1
South Carolina, 2, 20, 59
sovereignty, v, vi, xiii, xiv, xx, xxi, xxiv, 15, 24, 29, 31, 32, 33, 34, 35, 65, 68, 71, 82, 93, 94, 95, 97, 98, 99, 101, 102, 103, 104, 105, 108
Spirit Lake Tribe of North Dakota, 97
Standing Rock Sioux Tribe of South Dakota, 97
Stokes Smith Ceremonial Grounds, 23
Sturm, Circe, 32
Sunray, Cedric, 101, 103
Tahlequah OK, 15, 22, 23, 29
Tamiami Trail, 72
Tampa Bay FL, 81
Texas, 59, 60, 63, 74, 80, 86, 88, 89, 90
Texas-Indian Wars, 89
Third Seminole War, 71
Thomas-Rogers Act. *See* Oklahoma Indian Welfare Act of 1936
Tommie, Jack, 73
Treaties with C.S.A., 7
Treaty of 1805, 106

Treaty of 1866, iii, vi, vii, viii, xv, 5, 7, 8, 11, 25, 27, 28, 30, 39, 42, 43, 45, 48, 51, 65, 68, 70, 77, 78, 108
tribal rolls, xvii, 11, 12, 28, 42, 45, 46, 47, 48, 56, 57, 69, 72, 76, 95, 96, 106
Tulsa World newspaper, 25
University of Arkansas at Little Rock, 28
University of Texas, 74
Vann plantation, 20, 21
Vann, Edward "Ned", 19
Vann, James, 19, 20
Virginia General Assembly, 3
Wakokiye Tallassee Ceremonial Grounds, 23
War of 1812, 6
Washington D.C., v, 40, 42, 48, 55, 56, 57, 69, 80, 83, 95, 98
Wea people, 13
Webbers Falls OK, 20
Westo Tribe, 2
Wewoka OK, 57, 85, 86
white Cherokee, xiv, 35
Wichita people, 7
Wickliffe, George, 29
Wilkins, David, 98
Wilma Mankiller, ii, x, xxiii, 35
World War I, 15
Yamasee people, 40, 82

www.ingramcontent.com/pod-product-compliance
Lightning Source LLC
Chambersburg PA
CBHW060140100426
42744CB00007B/844